Thank you!
Victoria

This memoir stands as a testament to Dr. Victoria Johnson's exceptional journey, offering readers a deep dive into the life of a remarkable surgeon and an even more impressive human being.
– *Literary Titan*

A faith-driven story that will serve as high inspiration for women…A memoir that cultivates a warm, encouraging, honest tone about the process of re-envisioning life and purpose on many different levels.
– *Midwest Book Review*

RECOMMENDED – *The US Review of Books*

ISBN: 978-1-957262-80-2
From Trophy Wife to Cosmetic Surgeon

Copyright © 2023 by Victoria Johnson, M.D.
All rights reserved.

No part of this publication may be reproduced, distributed, or transmitted in any form or by any means, including photocopying, recording, or other electronic or mechanical methods, without the prior written permission of the publisher, except in the case of brief quotations embodied in critical reviews and certain other noncommercial uses permitted by copyright law.

For permission requests, write to the publisher at the address below.

Yorkshire Publishing
1425 E 41st Pl
Tulsa, OK 74105
www.YorkshirePublishing.com
918.394.2665

Printed in Canada

From Trophy Wife to Cosmetic Surgeon

Victoria Johnson, M.D.

Yorkshire Publishing
TULSA

This book is dedicated to my daughter, Elena Victoria, for standing by me all those years, for being quiet and patient so I could study, for wiping my tears when necessary, and for laughing with great joy as we both earned my degree.

Dr Vicky
By Joe W Johnson
July 3, 1997

This tried to be a poem,
But missed the warmth of her smile.
This tried to be a song,
But missed the lilt of her laughter.
This tried to be a blue sky morning,
But missed her sparkling spirit.
This tried to be the dark of night,
And there it found its mark.
Within the caverns of my heart
Memories of her are etched
Cave paintings
Revisited, discovered.
In this dark, I hear
The exultant song of a calling bird,
Announcing to the old gods,
The coming of a medicine woman.

PART I

"Tupelo"

"And a woman having an issue of blood twelve years, which had spent all her living upon physicians, neither could be healed of any came behind him, and touched the border of his garment: and immediately her issue of blood stanched and Jesus said, 'Who touched me?'" (Luke 8:43-48 KJV)

In the 1980s I was a housewife in Tupelo, Mississippi. My husband and I had an eight-year-old daughter who was in the third grade.

We had a very nice home on the golf course, but there wasn't much for me to do. I had previously owned different businesses, and being a stay-at-home mom was not for me. I became increasingly restless, had trouble sleeping, and felt this tremendous drive to get out and do something—but what? That question kept coming up.

My husband was terribly abusive and belittling. I hated that my daughter saw the abuse, but I was trapped. I found out later that my husband kept me that way on purpose and that he had been gaslighting me (beating me emotionally so that I would question my own sanity). It worked. I had no self-esteem and struggled with anorexia and bulimia.

The pain and sadness that I carried weighed me down like heavy boots and continued relentlessly for many years, as did my husband's attacks. I was miserable and hopeless.

I had heard that once the pain becomes intolerable, you break and change it. This correlated to a story a friend told me of how a mother eagle would get her grown chicks out of the nest: she would keep putting rocks and twigs in the nest to make them so uncomfortable that they had no choice but to leave. *Hmm*, I thought.

It was also in that time frame that Michael Jackson released the song "Man in the Mirror." I took the lyrics to heart and would stare at myself in the mirror, hating the image. I had to find a way to escape the pain.

When I was twenty-eight, I decided I needed to see a plastic surgeon to take care of a small problem that I thought I had. I had flawless skin, but that didn't reflect how I saw myself.

I made the appointment in Tupelo with a female plastic surgeon. Driving up to her office, I was mesmerized. She had her own building and out back was a playground for her twins.

After checking myself in, I waited to be called back. As I sat there, I became very agitated. When I was finally called back, I walked down the hallway, which was lined with her diplomas. I went by them slowly and read each one. Daggers pierced my heart, and I could barely stand to be there. I didn't dare think that I could have those diplomas too. My husband would never allow it!

Over the next weeks I reflected upon my experience at the doctor's office. Somehow, in my heart, my resolve grew. In the meantime, I suggested to my husband that we go to a marriage counselor. To my complete shock, he agreed, and I set up the appointment.

We drove to the counselor together, and my husband immediately took over the conversation. The counselor and I couldn't get a word in sideways.

My husband said I was crazy, unloading his vile attacks in front of the counselor. He screamed about how horrible I was, saying he knew the counselor would see it too. I was so embarrassed and humiliated that I just sat there silently. The counselor stood up, pointed his finger at my husband, and said that he wouldn't treat a dog the way my husband treated me. That did not go well with my husband. He got up and told me to come with him.

"We aren't coming back here," he said, and we drove home in silence.

I couldn't believe that the counselor stood up to my husband. I was so afraid of him that I thought everyone else was too. I decided to make another appointment with this counselor. Maybe he could help me have the strength to stand up to my husband. I proceeded to see "our marriage counselor" weekly for four years. I did get stronger and braver over time. The drive to change my life was overwhelming; it couldn't be stopped.

My faith in the Lord was strong, and I devoted time every day to praying and studying his word. Surely, he would provide an answer. I was determined to find out what it was.

I read every self-help book I could get my hands on and began fasting and praying every day for weeks. I would spend many hours on my knees seeking answers.

One morning I was so desperate for guidance and an answer that I got on my knees and cried out, "Lord, I am grabbing hold of the hem of your robe, and I am not letting go until you heal and answer me."

I was afraid that I had gone too far, but then I felt something brush my leg. I reluctantly opened my eye just a sliver to see what was touching me. I saw Jesus's sandals and his robe touching my leg as he walked by.

I then saw in my mind the foundation of a great building, and it lay cracked and broken. I then heard a tremendous crashing sound, and I watched as the foundation was made whole. I felt something in my spirit heal. A great peace fell over me, and I was reminded of a verse from Philippians: "And the peace of God, which surpasses all understanding, will guard your hearts and minds in Christ Jesus" (4:7 CSB). I also realized that a great rock—solid and immovable—was inside my chest. My foundation was made whole.

I continued fasting and praying, waiting for guidance from the Lord. One night, I was awakened by a noise that sounded as if someone was in my living room. I looked next to me—my husband was sleeping there. I heard the noise again!

Reluctantly I put on my robe and walked silently to my living room. There was no one physically there, but I felt a great presence. Humbled, I fell to my knees. In my mind I heard a voice say, "You are going to be a doctor!" Then peace fell on the room and me like a great wave, and I began to sob. The idea that I would become a doctor was impossible.

The last time I'd been in school was eleven years prior when I took a couple business courses at a community college. The idea scared me; my husband would never allow it. Then the questions started: How would I pay for it? How would I take care of my family, attend college, and study? How would I tell my husband? I was extremely afraid of him!

I found, however, a great tenacity growing inside me. I became committed to what the Lord had said to me: "You are going to be a doctor!"

Knowing he had to have a plan and a path for me, I was going to go for it. I wouldn't tell my husband until I had a plan and a way of executing it.

I called my sister Laurie, who was attending law school at Ole Miss. She agreed to hear me out and help me. She took me to the premed advisor, who was very kind as I told her about my husband and my situation at home. She came up with a schedule that would allow me to take care of my daughter and get her to and from school. I was so overwhelmed, but she said to me, "How do you eat an elephant?" I shook my head, at a loss. "One bite at a time," she said.

Next was the issue of money. How was I going to pay for this schooling?

My sister told me we should go to the bursar's office to see if I qualified for any financial assistance. A lovely man greeted us, and I explained my quandary. He led us into his office and smiled. "This is the first year that a married woman can borrow money for school without her husband's consent," he said. Wow! The schedule was working out and now I was able to borrow money on my own to finance my education. It would take me ten years to pay it off, but I knew I could do it. Everything was falling into place. Now I had to tell my husband.

I spent the next few days in prayer as I waited for the right opportunity. I made my husband his favorite dinner, and we had a nice meal. He was in a good mood, and I decided that this was the right time for me to tell him of my plan. It went as I expected with a torrent of verbal abuse. I was becoming somewhat numb to his attacks because my resolve was unshakeable. He threatened to take my car away and leave me with no access to money, but I already had no access to money, which weakened his threat.

He wouldn't stand in my way.

CHAPTER ONE

"Ole Miss"

I enrolled in my first semester at Ole Miss (the University of Mississippi), taking on a schedule of twelve hours of coursework that my premed counselor and I had worked out. My sister took me around campus to help me find my classes, and she made sure that I purchased the correct course books and other materials.

I woke at five each morning for my daily devotion, followed by a five-mile run. I then got my daughter ready for school, dropped her off, and headed to Oxford for class. My daughter and I had fun together. My sister had two children that were around Elena's age, so we hung out with them. I took Elena to baseball and football games, and we spent time in the beautiful old library on campus. (Like me, she came to acquire a taste for the smell of a library.) She read and drew while I studied.

I attended my classes, studied in between them, and then drove back to Tupelo to pick up my daughter from school. When I returned home, I took care of my house and cooked dinner.

I couldn't study in front of my husband because he would become so enraged that I was in school that it was impossible to concentrate. Instead, I started waking at three in the morning, giving myself a few hours to study. I would catch another hour or two to study when my husband played golf or was at work.

My daughter was only eight at the time but she was very supportive. She went to school with me from time to time and sat quietly during the lectures, coloring with her crayons the whole time. Her favorite thing was going to the Lyceum, where they had a cafeteria. She was amazed by the number of food choices there, but she almost always chose a bologna sandwich, chips and a Coke.

We also went to a local bookstore and coffee shop, sipping decaf lattes as I studied. I loved introducing her to college and wanted her to have a positive experience with school.

While she was growing up, when someone filled our tank at the station with gas, or when a waitress served us at a restaurant, I pointed out that that person had not gone to college. I know I was brainwashing my kid, but I thought it was important for her as a young girl growing up in the Deep South to get a higher education. Ole Miss had a reputation as a matchmaking market, a place where young women attended college to meet a rich or financially up-and-coming husband.

I did not want that for her. I wanted to demonstrate to her that a woman could make her own way in this world without a husband. I wanted to show her that a woman could become financially independent.

I had been so beaten down by my husband, and I hated that I had let her see how to survive in an abusive relationship. But that was where I was, and I would fight as hard as I could to be a better role model.

At the time, women's rights were not very good, and the "good ole boy club" was in full control. I tried several times to hire a lawyer to divorce my husband, but no one would let me. My husband had too much power. I was stuck for the time being, but I would make the best of it to obtain my goal.

"Our" marriage counselor helped me tremendously over the next four years, navigating my abusive marriage, as well as college and raising my daughter. (I keep saying "my" daughter instead of "our" daughter because my husband would later abandon her.)

For some reason after my husband's tantrum at our counselor's office, he was a little less mean, which translated to him no longer freaking out when he saw me studying. That was a big relief to at least have that freedom.

The days went by, and test after test, I was embarrassed to find myself failing in every subject; I had an average of 42 percent at mid-semester. I couldn't do the required math. I was so worried that my husband would find this out and laugh at my attempt at college and that I would be trapped again under his complete control.

I asked my sister for help. She showed me how to write in such a way that I was able to get my grades up in Composition 1. I then found a math tutor who saved my bacon. I met with her a few times a week and my college algebra and chemistry scores dramatically increased. I solved each problem in the workbooks thirty times until my math was up to college par.

The first exam I took after the midterms was in chemistry, a class I was failing, and I scored a 92 percent. I was so proud of myself that I went to my professor to show him. He was so excited for me. I told him that I'd had to learn how to do the math since I hadn't been in school for years. He then told me that he would wipe out all my previous scores and give me an A for the course!

Hope swelled in my chest as I took all the tests in my other courses. I finished my first semester of premed college with straight A's.

I never knew that I was smart.

I continued my track of straight A's every semester except the last one when I did receive a few B's. I didn't care though. I had to take twenty-five hours for the last two semesters! I was on track, but I had another huge obstacle to overcome.

I had to take the Medical College Admission Test (MCAT), which assumed that you had taken all the required premed courses. I hadn't, but if I didn't take the test that year, I wouldn't be able to apply to medical school for another year.

I went again to see my premed advisor, who was always kind and upbeat. I explained that I would not have my second semester of physics and organic chemistry before the test rolled around. We looked at my transcripts and couldn't find any way around having to take another year of classes.

I didn't want to tell her that things at home were worsening, and my husband was selling his business and would need to find another job, which might force me to leave school.

We decided that I should take a preparatory MCAT course to help me get ready for the test. I finished the course and applied to take the exam. I was not ready, but I thought it would be a good exercise for the next time I took it.

The day of the test was upon me. I rented a hotel room near the college where I tried to get some sleep. It was no use. I stayed up all night with visions of failure and my husband gloating over me.

I showed up at the test site where some of my friends were taking the exam too. I felt comforted that I had a few allies in my endeavor. I felt so old and inadequate. *Oh well!* I thought. *I've come this far!*

I took my time and did my best on the test. I would have to wait eight weeks to find out the results. At that time, I didn't know that my MCAT score would determine whether I received an invitation from a medical school to interview for admission into their school.

I just kept my head buried in my studies and plowed through my courses. There were only eighteen hours of prerequisite courses for medical school, so that left me with over 100 hours to complete a Bachelor of Arts. I needed only two more chemistry courses to receive a minor in chemistry.

I decided to take an anthropology course, which was the only one that I could plug into my packed semester. I fell in love with it! I interviewed my anthropology professor, and he really piqued my interest in pursuing a major in the field. I always loved Native American history books and novels, so this was a perfect course of action for me.

Eight weeks crawled by as I anxiously awaited my MCAT scores. I check the mailbox several times a day to see if my score had arrived.

Finally a small envelope arrived for me from the MCAT board. My heart was racing, and I thought I would throw up. I retrieved the envelope and walked nervously around and around the post office while my husband waited in the car. He had insisted upon going to see if I got my score.

I was so scared because I would have to tell him the results. He would be mad if my score was good or bad. He would be waiting with the appropriate response of nonsupport.

I made myself sit down on a small bench in the Tupelo post office and open the letter. Inside the envelope was a single sheet of paper with my information on it, and in the middle of the page it had in bold print "Passed," along with my score. I had obsessed over the score I would need to qualify for an interview. My score was so good that I remember thinking it had to be a joke—but it wasn't. I had overcome this hurdle and taken one more step closer to medical school.

I braced for my husband's response as I told him the good news. He didn't get upset at all and said that he was proud of me! *What?* I didn't know what had gotten into him, but he was supportive…for a while.

At that time, for entrance to medical school, you needed high scores in your premed coursework and you had to have your bachelor's degree. Then the MCAT score followed and you applied to medical schools. Then came in-person interviews with the various colleges. I decided to apply to several schools and see if I received any offers.

I received letters of invitation to interview at Tulane, Emory, University of Florida, and Ole Miss medical schools. I would then be offered a spot in each of their colleges to begin medical school the next fall. OH MY GOD!

I received my first letter of acceptance from Ole Miss's medical school in Jackson, Mississippi, on my thirtieth birthday. I raced to tell my husband, and lo and behold, he had flipped back to his mean self and berated me for hours. After he went to bed, I called my parents and told them that I had been accepted into medical school. They were ecstatic. My mom was the dean of a prominent nursing school, and my dad was a music professor.

I never had much of a relationship with my mother. She was English and very stout and proper. When I was a teenager, she once told me that I was amounting to nothing and she didn't know why I bothered with life. So when I called about my acceptance to Ole Miss and she and I talked for what seemed like hours, that conversation and her support really helped heal our relationship.

In the meantime, my husband had sold his business and accepted a position with an Oklahoma City car dealer to be the general manager. I had two more semesters to complete and was terrified that I would have to quit school.

To my complete surprise my husband said that he was moving to Oklahoma City and would get a small place so that we would have a place to stay when we came for a visit. I couldn't believe it. My daughter and I stayed behind to finish our school year. It was so wonderful not having my husband around. I could study and live in peace. I was getting closer to freedom.

At first, my husband called several times a day to check on me, but I noticed over time that he was calling less and less. I figured he probably had a girlfriend, but I didn't know and certainly did not care. Several months went by before I saw him again.

The semesters whizzed by, and I earned my undergraduate degree in two and a half years with a grade point average of 3.86. I received my Bachelor of Arts with a major in anthropology and a minor in chemistry from Ole Miss.

Besides receiving my degree, I met many wonderful people and made many friends. Life was getting better. I had borrowed the maximum possible for school loans and hoarded any extra money in a safety deposit box for emergencies.

I would need every penny.

CHAPTER TWO

"Oklahoma"

My husband began calling me again. He said he missed me and my daughter and asked if I would travel to Oklahoma City to visit him. I reluctantly agreed because my daughter was missing her father too.

My daughter was a great driving companion during the nine-hour trip from Tupelo to Oklahoma City. We each rented two books on tape and rotated them. It made the drive go by faster, and we both got to listen to our favorite books.

Once we arrived in OKC, we were surprised by the lack of trees and how big the sky looked. It was also very windy!

Our visit went well. My husband was on his best behavior, and we really had fun as a family.

Then the lobby began. My husband explained that I should move to OKC and apply to the medical school there, saying we could reconcile and get back together. I hadn't known we were apart. At first, my fear and suspicion overwhelmed me, but after several nice visits with him, coupled with my daughter pleading with me for us to move back with her father, I agreed to investigate the possibility.

I had no idea how I would get into medical school in Oklahoma City. I had already been accepted to other medical schools and was weighing which one I would attend when this came up. I decided to call the University of Oklahoma College of Medicine and ask them for advice.

I spoke with Susan Massara, a lovely, bubbly lady, who instantly put me at ease. I explained my problem, and she said that people move all the time and she would see what she could do. She wanted me to send her my transcripts and test scores along with the acceptance letters I had received from the other schools.

I sent everything to her one morning, and by that afternoon I had a letter of acceptance to the University of Oklahoma College of Medicine! Wow! I hadn't planned on this.

My husband and daughter were ecstatic, and I had to cave in. We decided to sell our home in Tupelo and move.

This change in our situation relieved me a little. I would at least have some help with my daughter.

It would be six more weeks before medical school started, so we explored Oklahoma City and got familiar with where everything was.

Each day I drove to the medical school campus, parked outside the entrance doors, and just stared at them. I was so scared but exhilarated at the same time. I was one more step closer to becoming a doctor!

MEDICAL SCHOOL

Before I could attend school, I was required to take a cardiopulmonary resuscitation course that the College of Medicine had arranged for first-year medical students. I had taken one of these courses many years ago, but I sure needed a refresher.

I went to the classroom where the course was held and felt very out of place. Many of the medical students already had a medicine or nursing background. Thankfully I was paired with Joan Hardt, who would be attending first year with me. We became dear, fast friends. She shared with me her own fears of medical school and of being overwhelmed.

The first day of medical school was finally here. I arrived early and picked up my classroom assignments. After Joani got hers, we met for coffee and compared where we would be.

They split the class of 124 into ten modules that were all together on the second floor of the building. Joani and I discovered we were not in the same module. We went to the admissions office and asked if we could be reassigned so that we were together for our classes. They said it was no problem and placed us in the same module and on the same cadaver for anatomy class.

I had never seen a dead body before the first day of anatomy. I was worried how it would affect me. The class was in the basement of the building, and there were sixty to seventy metal, coffin-looking boxes that were about waist-high and filled with formaldehyde. The lids were closed, but our bodies—men and women—were inside them in clear plastic bags.

The teachers did a great job introducing us to our body. On each bag was a very nice biography of the person we were going to dissect. Our cadaver was a very large man who had been in great shape. He had been a farmer in his life, with a family and grandchildren. I don't remember the details, but knowing a little about him made Joan and me less nervous. We both felt grateful that this man donated his body so that we could learn anatomy.

After we completed our dissection assignment for the day, we submerged our body back into the formaldehyde and closed the lid. The smell in the room was so powerful that it stayed in our clothes for hours. I would go home and immediately take a shower and wash my clothes.

The classes were fascinating, and I felt the knowledge soaking into my brain. My heart was full. This was where I was meant to be.

HOME

It didn't take long for my husband to begin demanding that I come home on time from school to cook his dinner and take care of my family. I explained to him that I had no control over my hours and was in no position to ask for favors to leave to make his dinner.

The hours weren't bad the first year, except the hours of studying were intense. I loved every moment and felt my confidence building.

Joan was great! She was such a good influence on me. She was strong, raising two sons by herself while attending school. Her boys were around my daughter's age, so it was easy to get together and study while they entertained themselves.

The day came when we were to attend a party at a fellow student's home, and I was to bring my husband. I didn't know how he would react to being around my fellow classmates, so I was apprehensive.

The party was fun and some of the other students brought their significant others. I couldn't believe that I was finally around like-minded, serious students. Again, my confidence in myself continued to grow.

We weren't at the party long before my husband began to humiliate me in front of the others. I think that he thought he could convince them that I was crazy and stupid and that I didn't belong.

I was so torn down and wanted to run out of the room when Joani came to my defense. She told my husband that she would not put up with him treating me this way and that he was the one that appeared crazy. Some of the other women in my class agreed, and my husband left. This happened a few more times at gatherings with my classmates. Finally, he stopped attending them with me.

I was fine with that.

I began standing up for myself at home and demanded that he help with my daughter and cook his own dinner if I was still at school.

Things were not going well for him. I was succeeding in school, and by the end of the first year, I was in the top of my class. He hated it. Each test I took was one more step toward freedom from abuse.

BID FOR INDEPENDENCE

Every year we sent our daughter to a camp in Alabama, and every year she really flourished. She came back stronger and more confident each time she went. I wanted to make sure that she attended camp again this year.

I started working with my lawyer who had no problem confronting my husband and helping me file for divorce. We decided to file while my daughter was at camp.

The day came when my husband and I drove to the airport with my daughter to meet a group of people who were also flying out to camp. On the way back home, I told him that I had filed for divorce. The ride home was filled with his usual barrage of attacks on me. I was undeterred. This had to end.

I was successful in medical school; I was going to be successful in life! My daughter and I were no longer going to live with this abuse!

After we got home, I spoke with my lawyer, and he informed me that I had to live with my husband for six more weeks in the same house before a court date could be obtained. He continued his job, and I continued to go to school. It was extremely uncomfortable. He would not leave. Each evening we just ignored each other. Even though he wasn't as abusive as he had been, it was still very stressful, and it was difficult to rest.

I just pressed on with my studies and waited out the six weeks. We finally got a court date, and a judge assigned child support and alimony and settled all the other details.

My husband decided to take a job in New Orleans with an old business associate, and one day shortly after court, he left!

I remember the last time I saw him. I didn't even wave. My daughter was standing beside me, seemingly unmoved. We were relieved that we were getting some closure and relief from the abuse.

The days went on, and I took care of my daughter. I took her—and myself—to and from school. We both continued to do well in our studies and enjoyed a peaceful home for a while.

A period of time went by, and my husband wanted my daughter to come to New Orleans for a visit during a school break. She was to stay for a week. I let her go, and he refused to send her back to me.

I wouldn't see her for a year.

My daughter was the most important person in my life, and I wasn't allowed to even speak to her.

"I told you I'd make you flunk out of medical school!" my husband said.

I was miserable. My anxiety became so overwhelming that it crippled me. I knew I couldn't go on like that. I decided that when I wasn't in school or studying, I would become a serious runner again.

After a long, intense run, the anxiety would abate long enough for me to get some rest. I pushed my fear for my daughter down deep so that I could concentrate on my studies.

I tried repeatedly to call her, but my husband or his girlfriend always answered, telling me that my daughter wasn't allowed to speak to me. (Funnily enough, his girlfriend called me one day and wanted my recipe for chicken wings!)

One night, after my daughter had been gone about a year, I received a phone call from her, and she was panicked. I asked her what was going on. She said, "Mom, I'm not allowed to talk to you or call you. I'm at a friend's house and they let me call you!"

She went on to explain that her father's girlfriend would be staying at their house on the upcoming weekend and that she needed to find a place to stay for those days. He told her he didn't care where she went, but she had to get out.

I told her that I had a few days' break from school and that I was on my way to pick her up and bring her to Oklahoma City to live with me. When I arrived at their house, my daughter ran to me and held me for a long time, tears streaming from her eyes.

We were quickly met by my husband. During the eleven-hour drive from OKC to New Orleans, I mentally prepared to deal with him.

I was very cordial, but I whispered to my daughter that we had to hurry and pack her things and get out of there fast. My husband was very unpredictable, and I just wanted to get my daughter and her things and be back on the road to OKC.

We packed all that would fit in my small car and drove off. I showed no emotion toward my husband. I was calm and protective of my daughter, but everything went smoothly.

We had a great time driving back home. We talked and talked and laughed like we were happy again!

Her father didn't ask to see her again for many years.

My husband was supposed to pay me $450 in alimony a month and $1,000 or so in child support. A few months went by, and he paid me nothing. I was afraid that I wasn't going to be able to take care of my daughter. I spoke with my lawyer, and he told me that he could arrange for a bench warrant to be served on my husband demanding payment of the child support.

It worked like magic! He sent me what he owed me. For a while he paid the monthly sum, then he stopped again. He called me and told me that he had lost his job and was unable to pay me. Since he was over sixty-seven, I thought he was eligible for social security. (I don't remember why this thought came into my head, but it did.)

I called the social security office and made an appointment with a staff member there. Taking my daughter with me, we explained the situation and asked if my daughter was eligible to receive money on her father's social security account.

After looking into it, the staff member told me that my husband had been receiving around $700 a month for her from social security. I was shocked. He still wasn't paying me. She said that because my daughter was living with me, she would be able to send the money to me on her behalf. So that was that!

My husband must have gotten scared or something (who knows?) because he started paying me the $450 a month in alimony. He also started paying for a car for me. I just took it without question.

All my daughter and I had to live on was the excess that I borrowed on my school loans, which amounted to around $700 a month. The extra money helped a lot.

We moved into a small home in a portion of Oklahoma City called The Village where we lived for the next five years. We were very comfortable.

My daughter was so fabulous. One day she said, "Mom, I'm sixteen. I need to get a job." I agreed with her on that. She was doing well in school, and I had my first job, cleaning houses, when I was eight.

She got herself a job at a local Mexican restaurant that was only a few blocks from our house and her school. It was a good fit for her. She found out quickly that she was the only person in the restaurant that spoke English well, so they were very glad to have her.

One day at the restaurant their cash register stopped working, and they panicked. My daughter received her first computer when she was six and would spend hours and hours taking it apart and putting it back together. She became a master of the device. So when the cash register stopped working, my daughter stepped in, took it apart, and repaired it for them. They were so excited, and I was so proud. I hadn't realized that she could do that!

The first and second years of medical school passed, and I continued to thrive, as did my daughter. She was so supportive and kept herself out of trouble. I had wanted to put her in a private school, but there was no way I could afford it. So she went to a public school close to our house.

It turned out that she loved public school. She made many friends, and I was very glad for her. I made my house the "fun house." I wanted all her friends to know they were welcome. I kept snacks and drinks available, and I afforded us a small cable-access package. When some of her friends had episodes of instability at their homes, they stayed with us.

The third and fourth years of medical school whizzed by, and it was time to decide what I wanted to study in my residency. (In medicine, you can't get your full medical license until you complete an internship in any discipline that you chose.)

I was trying to decide in which area I would like to focus my career. I was interested in emergency medicine, obstetrics and gynecology, and family medicine.

The time came for "match" to occur, and I had to decide. I remember having twenty minutes in front of a computer, and I had to choose. I finally decided to choose family medicine. I thought I was going to be a doctor in a small town, and I could still do emergency and OB/GYN.

I think my daughter was in the eleventh grade when I started my intern year of residency. I had applied to match in Oklahoma City so that my daughter would not have to change schools. My goal was to keep her in one place if possible so that she felt some stability in her life.

She became very independent, which was a blessing because the hours were very long, and I was on call a great deal of the time. We lived in a safe neighborhood, and our house had an alarm as well. I had also purchased a small used car for my daughter. Many times, while I was on call or working long hours, she came to visit me, and we had dinner in the hospital cafeteria.

When I finished my fourth year of medical school, it was time for graduation. My daughter and I went to the ceremony, and when I walked across the stage, she shouted, "Way to go, Mom!" and everyone cheered! I was so proud of both of us.

She graduated from high school shortly after that and enrolled in college. She would eventually move in with some of her friends. She always had at least one job and went to college.

Residency went by, and my confidence grew. I loved medicine! I had excellent professors that were patient with new doctors.

The *practice* of medicine is just that. You practice and practice while seeing your patients. I loved the challenge of trying to find out what was wrong with each patient and what was the appropriate treatment course. Sometimes I just had to guess.

After my intern year, I received my full medical license and was ready to roll. I had been on a rotation in a small town where I was assigned to an old pediatrician. Just two weeks before my rotation was to begin, his son was killed in an automobile accident. I was worried he was not going to want me to be there, but he said come on anyway.

Dr. Orr was a local celebrity and a well-respected pediatrician. He had short white hair and wore a black bow tie with his white coat each day at clinic.

I followed him from room to room at his very busy practice. He complimented me on my bedside manner and eventually allowed me to see his patients first and then report to him.

One day during the lunch break I went into his office as usual, and his head was on the desk. He had been crying. I started to leave to allow him some privacy, but he waved for me to come in.

He lifted himself off the desk and straightened his tie and coat. Then he put on the biggest fake smile. "Some days you just put on your game face," he said, and then clinic began again.

I will never forget his kindness and strength that he showed me. I never forgot this experience. Doctors are regular people too. We suffer personal loss and troubles just like everyone else.

"Some days you just put on your game face!"

This was a powerful lesson.

EMERGENCY MEDICINE

I had been able to take many rotations in the emergency department, and since I had my medical license, as well as other appropriate licenses, I was going to ask for a job at the ER in that small town.

There I met Dr. Storms, who oversaw the emergency department at that hospital for many years. I introduced myself and explained where I was in my training. He hired me and paid me the same money as the other physicians who also worked there. When he told me how much I was to make an hour, I almost passed out. I don't remember the number, but to me it was a fortune.

Dr. Storms was such a great mentor. He was always available to answer my questions and help me with difficult patients, and he was always positive and supportive.

I worked as many shifts as I could and still attended my residency program. My shifts were 6 p.m. to 6 a.m. Occasionally I would get some sleep on my shift, but no matter; I had to be prepared for the day at school and in the hospitals.

When I arrived for my first shift in the ER, the physician who worked the shift before me introduced himself. He then handed me a chart with an electrocardiogram that showed a man with an acute myocardial infarction (heart attack).

I tried not to panic, and I took a deep breath. I studied the chart and then went to see the patient. We had to work fast to get him stabilized and ready for transfer to a hospital where he could undergo heart surgery or other procedures that were not performed at that hospital. I ordered the appropriate treatment and then sent him by ambulance for further treatment.

Years later, I was standing outside somewhere, and a gentleman approached me, sticking out his hand. I was confused. I didn't recognize him. He said, "Dr. Johnson, you saved my life and I wanted to thank you!" His grip was very powerful, and his gratitude was heartfelt.

Wow! That blew me away.

I had many wonderful and scary times in the emergency room. I learned a lot about what to do and what not to do when taking care of patients. The nurses were fun, and we found ways to make the shifts fun. I learned so much from them, and I thank them for their patience with me. I so appreciated their gentle guidance as they saw me struggle with the appropriate care of patients.

Another powerful mentor was Linda Johnson, MD. She was the first female surgeon in Oklahoma, and she was tough as nails.

One day I had a patient with abdominal pain. I evaluated the patient and ordered the appropriate tests and X-rays. When I received all the results, I found the patient had an issue with his colon.

I called Dr. Johnson in to consult with the patient. It was our first meeting, and I was nervous about what she might say about my diagnosis for this patient.

After a while, the door to the ER opened, and a small middle-aged woman sauntered in, wearing a white lab coat and a stethoscope around her neck.

"Dr. Johnson?" she asked. Then she introduced herself.

We began discussing the results I had obtained about the patient. I noticed Dr. Johnson was wearing an old, dirty T-shirt; jeans; and muck-covered work boots. She had been shoveling out her barn and just came right in when I called her. Everywhere she walked, she left a trail of muck.

I showed her the way to the patient's room. She walked very slowly and deliberately, which relaxed me and increased my confidence. She was so calm as she listened to my diagnosis for the patient.

After looking at the patient's X-ray image for a few minutes, she said, "Dr. Johnson, I can see why you diagnosed this patient as you did, but if you were to look at this part of the X-ray, you can see that perhaps this is actually the diagnosis."

As she was explaining why my diagnosis was incorrect, she said, "Good job, you're right that this patient has a surgical abdomen and needs to go to surgery now!"

We smiled at each other. She put her hand on my shoulder and said, "Welcome to medicine!"

I would have many more encounters with Dr. Johnson, and each one taught me so much.

One night we got a visit from a local policeman. I had seen him many times; he brought me prisoners to treat, or he came to pick them up. He slowly entered my area, walking very rigid. I asked him if he was OK, and he shook his head no.

I asked him what the matter was, and he said he was having excruciating abdominal pain and could barely breathe. He went on to explain that he had been in a fight with a prisoner the night before and received several blows to stomach.

I asked him if he would change into a gown, but he said he couldn't move. All he would let me do was obtain lab work and gently touch his abdomen. I immediately knew that he needed surgery now, but I did not know the cause.

Again, I called Dr. Johnson to help take care of the patient.

She sauntered in with her quiet strength and wearing her usual attire. She was never rattled. I explained the problem that the policeman was having and that he wouldn't undress. She examined his abdomen and agreed that he needed surgery now. She escorted him to the operating room.

My shift was busy, and I had forgotten all about the policeman when I received an overhead page. "Dr. Johnson, please see Dr. Linda Johnson in surgery!"

I was surprised, but I was at a stopping place in the ER, so I went up to see what was going on. They had to give the policeman anesthesia to get his clothes off and prepare him for surgery.

I was waved through to the operating room where Dr. Johnson asked me to come and look in this patient's abdomen. I did, and she praised me for having diagnosed this rare form of infarcted (dead) bowel. The blows the patient suffered had cut off some of the circulation to a vital area of the abdomen.

I had gotten it right! She was proud of me. My face was beaming when I got back to the ER.

It was such an honor to work with Dr. Johnson. I always learned something from her. I think the most powerful thing I learned was not to panic and to stay completely calm while taking care of a critically ill patient or raging family members.

Dr. Johnson never hurried anywhere, no matter how desperate a patient's situation. She knew it was better to be the calmest, most confident person in the room.

Now when I am placed in a critical situation, I think, "What would Dr. Johnson do?" I mimic her slow-paced walk, and I talk slowly and deliberately. You can think clearly if you stay calm.

I worked in the ER for the next three years, taking as many shifts as possible. The ER was on a major turnpike and the only hospital for many small towns. The turnpike was very busy, and we received many patients who were victims of terrible automobile accidents. We also got our share of heart attacks and other critical situations.

My skills and confidence were growing, and I tried to be painstakingly thorough with my evaluation of each patient.

PRISONERS

My next shift in the emergency room was challenging. We received a prisoner from the local jail who was being held for trial. I barely paid attention to the details until the prisoner arrived. He was handcuffed and accompanied by two officers. The nurses guided them to the exam room where he was chained to the bed.

The nurses came into the doctors' area and were excitedly trying to tell me this prisoner's history. I put down the chart I was working on to give them my attention. These women were not easily rattled, but they were on this occasion.

"What's this all about?" I asked.

The head nurse said that the prisoner was the person that authorities had found torturing and killing four small children after sexually assaulting them. The case was in the news everywhere, and I was concerned that I might incur a visit from a vigilante.

The prisoner had become angry in his cell and struck his fist against the concrete cell wall, suffering a "boxer's" fracture. He had broken bones in his hand, and I was to take care of him.

I went in to examine the prisoner, who was loud and abusive toward the staff and myself.

He finally agreed to an X-ray of his hand, from which I could plainly see the extent of his injuries. I planned to set a cast on his injured hand.

The nurses came to me and said that he was asking for something for pain. My response shocked me: all I could think of was those four dead children and how much pain they had suffered at this man's hands. I didn't know what to do. I spoke with the nurses and said we had to address this issue.

I decided I would give him two Tylenol. I then set his hand, and he was sent back to the jail. I still don't know if that was the right thing to do, but that was my decision.

I then received a married couple, recognizing the large man from past encounters when he was a prisoner. As I entered the room to examine my patient, the man was blocking the door. I moved him to the side and saw a small, frail young woman cowering on the exam table. Her face was swollen.

At that point the police came to take a report of the assault that this man had done to his wife.

I ordered the studies to be performed on this woman so that a diagnosis could be made. It was obvious from her X-rays that she had been punched in the face so hard that all the bones in her cheek were crushed.

The husband stood in front of me, glaring at me. I could see that he treated his wife the same way. I wanted to give her hope and help her be strong when confronted by this man.

Standing toe to toe with him and staring him in the eyes, I said that I was not afraid of him and that I could see that his wife had been struck with enough force to break her facial bones. I dared him to hit me that way, taunting him for a few moments, not fearing the consequences.

The woman stared at me, shock and fear clearly written on her face. I stood my ground, and finally the man moved away and took a seat.

I could relate to this woman and many others that I cared for. I wanted to show her that her husband wasn't as scary as he made out to be.

The police arrested him and took him away, and I got a social worker to come and help this woman find a place to stay and begin to heal.

MY FIRST REAL JOB AS A PHYSICIAN

The time came for me to graduate from residency and look for a job. I had worked closely with the physicians that practiced in that area, and for the most part they treated me with respect and patience.

One day, the hospital administrator called me, saying he wanted to speak with me about a job offer. I was a bit nervous as I sat there waiting for him. Then he came through the door and excitedly asked me if I wanted a job at one of their clinics associated with the hospital. He said he was preparing an agreement for me to sign, and I was to begin immediately.

I had signed an agreement back in residency that the state would send me $1,000 a month for three years, and in return I would be obligated to practice in a small town for the same amount of time. I thought working for three years in this community would be just fine. I already knew the doctors, and I knew how the hospital worked. I thought that it would be a great fit, and the money they offered me was—to me at the time—astronomical!

My graduation ceremony was very moving. After many, many years of medical training I was very emotional and grateful to all that participated in my education.

As I reflected on that time, I realized that the attending physicians (the physicians that trained us) gave so much of themselves. Sure, they were getting paid to train us, but it seemed so much more. They cared for us as people, as students, and as colleagues. They shared their personal experiences and struggles with us. There are ups and downs to practicing medicine, and it's important to remember that you are "practicing" medicine. There are many aspects to caring for and interacting with patients and their families, which was one of the things that drew me to family medicine—the care of the whole family as well as the patient and their situation.

I will always be grateful to Dr. Zubialde, Dr. Brand, Dr. Sparks, Dr. Crawford, and countless others, as well as to the countless support staff that were there for me and taught me how to be a competent, caring physician.

Most importantly, I want to thank my dearest friend Dr. William Cook. He allowed me to rotate with him several months when I was an intern and resident; he is still my trusted friend in life. He not only taught me medicine but allowed me to practice with him as a colleague. His devotion to medicine and education is still intensely passionate as he continues to practice well into his seventies.

It was finally time to begin my personal professional career. In my contract, it stated that I had to live within thirty miles of the hospital because when I was on call, I would need to be able to be at the hospital quickly.

I was able to find a vacant lot within those parameters and purchased it. I was going to build my first house by myself. The owners of the development were a couple of young enthusiastic men that were a joy to work with.

I went to the bank and asked how much I would be able to borrow to build the house. They gave me an amount, and I met with the builders again. They had several floor-plan and budget options. I chose a floor plan that fitted what I wanted and could afford.

I put my house in Oklahoma City up for sale and started planning how I would decorate my new home. I spent many hours of my downtime pouring through design books and paint swatches. It was a magical time. I was very scared, but mostly I was very happy and content.

I arose each morning at five and worked out for an hour or so before getting to that hospital to make rounds or get ready for the day. I was very confident in my abilities as a physician, but I didn't know the inner workings of the clinic where I was working.

This lack of knowledge landed me in conflict with the manager, who was very happy to point out the errors of my ways. I had never worked in this kind of environment and didn't know the subtle rules.

One day, she said that she had "written me up" for wearing sandals to work. I had heard of nurses being written up but not a physician, so I really didn't know what it meant or where to go to find out what it meant.

I asked around about it and the "rules" that were unfamiliar to me. I met Collette Ellis, a wonderful woman who was the speech pathologist for the hospital. We became fast friends and still are to this day.

She had worked for many years in this environment and had much insight into what behaviors were acceptable, including attire. I always dressed professionally, but I found out there were different sets of rules for different groups of people.

I tried to conform as much as possible and stay out of trouble. The problem was that in the three years that I worked there, I made the mistake of seeing more patients and making more money than most of the older physicians. I thought that working hard and making money for the clinic was a good thing. I was wrong.

The clinic where I worked consisted of five middle-aged to older male physicians. Most of them were very nice and supportive, some not so much. I came to learn well what the term "good ole boy club" meant.

Usually when a physician at the clinic was on call, we would take care of the other physicians' patients for a period. We saw them as needed in the hospital and answered phone calls from the nurses or pharmacists. This was a common practice and allowed everyone some time off in the evenings and weekends or for vacation time.

I really hated the Monday morning after I had been on call. I called it the "Monday morning quarterbacks'" critique. Some of the physicians would complain to the nurses about how incompetent I was as a physician. They disagreed with my assessments and the courses of action I had taken with their patients over the weekend.

I understand that I was not as experienced as they were. After all, this was my first job. I never understood why, as my colleagues, they couldn't have just discussed the issues with me so that I better understood their frustration with my actions or orders. They didn't do this, so I would go back later and look at the charts of the patients in question. I never could find any glaring "crime" that would cause such anger in them against me.

One year, unknown to me, I was placed on the ballot for physician of the year in the local paper (I would later learn that the same physician had won for years in my category), and I won. I was never put on the ballot again, and the same old physician began winning again!

The weeks and months went by with many memorable happenings. I loved my patients and my home. Stress at work was hard on me, but I became stronger. I just kept my head down and worked as hard as I could.

I was relentless in my pursuit of medical knowledge and continued to study as if I were back in school. The thing about medicine is that you never really graduate. You never really finish learning and practicing.

I was working one Mother's Day when I was called to a patient's room where a family was gathered over their aged mother. They were crying. I had been asked to pronounce the patient dead. I was so moved by the scene, but I knew I had to act confidently while carrying out my job. I expressed my condolences and left the room.

I went back to my office and was collecting my emotions when I was called to the emergency room. There I found another family gathered by the bed of their matriarch. I thought, "What now?"

I picked up the chart and began reading. This patient had insisted on making the meal for her Mother's Day celebration. Her family was angry with her because they had insisted upon taking her out to lunch for the occasion. Evidently the patient had different ideas and had gone to the freezer to retrieve a large roast she intended to cook. When she picked up the roast, she dropped it on her foot, and the impact broke her bones.

I took appropriate steps to care for the patient, and she and the family left.

I then decided to get some lunch in the cafeteria at the hospital. They had the best food, especially their fried chicken. People came from everywhere to enjoy this crunchy treat.

I was finishing my lunch when the emergency room physician called me. We knew each other well and had worked together many times. He asked me if I would help in the ER because they were really backed up with patients, many of whom needed to be cared for immediately. I told him I would be there in just a few minutes.

Entering the ER department, I saw the long line of patients awaiting care. I was handed a chart by a frantic nurse with whom I had also worked many times. She asked me to see this patient immediately.

I had just sat down in the doctors' area and begun reading the chart when a young man came to stand next to me. He asked if I was going to take care of his mother. I said that I was just starting to review her chart and plan. His face registered his worry. He asked if he could be there when I cared for her. I didn't know what the right thing was to do. I hadn't seen the condition of his mother yet, but looking into this man's eyes, I motioned him to come with me. I had read enough of the chart to know this was not going to be a good prognosis.

Earlier in the day, the patient's family had taken her out for lunch at a local restaurant. The patient had insisted on driving the family to enjoy the meal. After the meal was over, her daughter-in-law insisted that she drive them home. The patient agreed and stayed behind while her daughter-in-law retrieved the car.

The family started toward the car, unbeknownst to the driver, who was backing up. The driver then accelerated to turn the car toward the family and struck the patient, causing a fatal brain injury.

When I entered the room to quickly assess the damage, I realized she needed to be placed on a ventilator. The young man stood motionless in the corner as I went about the treatment for his mother. I was able to stabilize her for transport to a larger hospital that would be able to take more intense care of her.

The young man came over to me as we loaded her into an ambulance, and he thanked me for helping his mother. We both had tears in our eyes as the ambulance moved away.

A few days later, he sent me a dozen roses. I was very moved. I later checked on how his mother had fared and was told she had passed away.

Medicine, as life, can be very hard. I will always remember that young man's face and the love that he had for his mother.

The next day came, and it was time to be assigned call for the next year. I asked the person in charge of the on-call schedule if it was possible for me not to work Mother's Day next year. They agreed. Whew!

POLITICS AND POWER

There was another lesson that I was to learn the hard way. After being employed at that clinic for about a year, I was summoned one day into the manager's office. I didn't think anything of it. I had stopped in her office many times for various reasons, including just to pass the time of day.

This time was different. As I sat down in the chair across from her desk, she glared at me. I asked what on earth was the matter. She explained that one of the major insurance companies had performed routine audits of my charts and that I had failed each audit.

"What audit?" I asked. "What are you talking about? And why was I not informed of the audit or the results before now?"

Her only response was that if I failed again, I would lose my privileges with the insurance company and, consequently, with the hospital and clinic.

I was flabbergasted! I had never been so blindsided in my life. She quickly ended the meeting as I tried to collect myself and get to my office. *Wow!* I thought. *They're trying to get rid of me.* If I lost my privileges, then my medical license could be in jeopardy.

I shared an office with three other doctors, so I had to be very measured in my next moments. Then I realized that a fellow physician that had been in my residency was the head of that division of the insurance company. We had a friendly relationship, so I called her and explained about the failed audits and the lack of notice that I was being audited.

She took a few moments and found the relevant information. She told me that the insurance company had given notice three times to the manager and that she picked the charts without my knowledge. My friend thought it was strange that I had failed three times.

She told me that she would send an auditor out on a particular day and that I could pick the charts to be audited. She also said that I could sit with the auditor, and they would show me what I had done right or wrong.

At that time insurance companies were implementing a systemized method of charting for billing purposes across the country. They wanted you to document all the procedures, results, diagnoses, etc. to justify your level of billing for reimbursement. It was a complicated system, and we were all struggling to get our heads around it.

The day came when the auditor was to visit, and I sat with him while he audited my charts. He showed me the items that he was looking for and the different elements that were necessary to justify a certain billing level. He then said that I passed. I spoke with him for a while and asked for more guidance. He handed me a couple sheets of paper and told me to follow these instructions when I was submitting my chart and the billing level.

Wow, I thought, *that was easy*. I now had a template I could use to help me stay out of future trouble. Why did the manager not give me one? My fear and anxiety skyrocketed. Were they trying to get rid of me and ruin my career in medicine? I kept to myself, trying not to interact too much with anyone but my nurse and patients. What else was in store for me?

Another incident occurred with a patient. I had my initial appointment with them and found a few health issues but nothing life-threatening. I soon forgot the encounter.

The patient came back in for a follow-up soon after the first appointment. Nothing special or new had happened with this patient, so I was confused as to why the patient was back. They had some minor complaints, and I reassured them that, from what I could see, they were in good health. The patient left.

This happened again for the next few days. I would see the patient, but the patient was getting more agitated and confused with each visit. I began to be afraid, and my gut said something was wrong. I then had my nurse accompany me with each visit.

One day, I heard a commotion at the front desk, and someone was shouting angrily at the receptionist, something about needing to see me.

I heard the receptionist explain that there were no available appointments with me that day, but she would gladly get the patient scheduled for a future date.

Then the door of the clinic flew open, and the patient stormed into the area where I see patients. The patient continued to scream obscenities and demand to see me.

I was scared. The patient had cornered me at my desk. Luckily one of the other physicians had been a Green Beret. He came over as the patient bolted toward me, and he performed self-defense maneuvers on this patient, finally subduing them.

The police were summoned, and the patient was led off to jail. I never saw the patient again.

I continued to work and take care of my patients. I worked with the receptionist to fulfill my goal of forty patients a day. I was younger and more energetic, and I always imposed a challenge on myself. I finally reached that goal and was satisfied.

My reputation was growing in the community, and people were attracted to my practice. My evaluations of each patient were thorough, and I became involved with them and had a special bond with some of them. I loved the practice of medicine.

Another day, when I arrived at the clinic, I was greeted by the manager. I interacted with her cheerily, and she asked if I would step into her office. I followed her and sat in my usual chair. I didn't think anything was wrong, so I was unconcerned.

She had a patient chart in her hand and asked me if I remembered the patient. I said that I did remember but would like to see the chart. I looked at it for a few minutes to make sure that I was familiar with it.

She then asked me why I had lied when I ordered a test for this patient.

"What?" I asked in dismay.

She went on to tell me that I had ordered a stress test on this patient for chest pain and that the patient had no chest pain.

I looked at the chart again and found the order sheet. I explained that I had ordered this test because of a family history of heart problems, and the patient had high blood pressure and elevated cholesterol. That was the justification, and it was correct.

She told me that on the order that went to the lab it showed I said the patient had chest pain. The physician performing the test wanted to let me know that that was Medicare fraud.

I looked at my order again and saw nothing that I had written or stated that indicated the patient had chest pain. After further investigation I was to learn that the nurse in the lab had added that later, and the physician just wanted me in trouble (that is what I was told from the people who worked in the lab).

They were trying to run me off, and this allegation could potentially ruin my career. I was so scared and alone. The only friend I had as a physician was Dr. Cook. He allowed me to call him about the care of certain patients that I would have in the ICU or elsewhere.

One day I called him from the ICU, and he said, "Now I know you aren't calling me to help you with a patient." I told him that I was, and he told me that I was a fine physician and that I did not need his help to treat my patients. It felt like a graduation to have been complimented in such a way from this incredibly respected physician.

I told him what was going on with the situation with the stress test. He was sad for me but not surprised. This medical community was notorious for running off new doctors.

I became almost frantic and spoke with Joan again. She had been practicing emergency medicine at a local hospital and gotten turned off by it. She had been searching for opportunities to turn her career in another direction.

Graduating High School 1976

Graduating Ole Miss

Med School Graduation Picture

Me at 19, which is when I got married

Me, (on the left) and my daughter. I'm 21, she is 18 months

Me, being silly

Me, at about 27

Just beginning my medical practice

Early morning pool work-outs

She had long been interested in having a clinic that treated varicose and spider veins. She had partnered with another physician, and they opened their own place. She also had an aesthetic laser and was doing Botox and wrinkle fillers, among other things.

I visited her one day at her clinic and was so impressed by the beauty of the place. It was so elegant yet professional. I had her provide me with some treatments. She is a very talented person.

I got to thinking, if Joan could make a break and change her career, then so could I.

I began researching the aesthetics market. There wasn't really anyone doing much online yet, but I managed to find a company that sold used lasers and that would help you set up your clinic and get you trained in different procedures.

I had many conversations with the owner, and he steered me in the right direction. He suggested a list of lasers and treatments that would be beneficial to my patients and profitable for me. After all, medicine is a business too, so the bottom line is that you must make money.

I spoke with friends and colleagues about a possible change in my career. As I learned more about the aesthetic space, I realized that it was just starting to be a viable market and there was plenty of room for new ideas and practices.

I traveled to Los Angeles where I met a physician who had been an anesthesiologist but had transitioned to aesthetics a few years ago. She taught me how to inject Botox and wrinkle fillers, and her nurse trained me on a few laser procedures.

I decided that I could make this move and make money. I knew that I could always moonlight in the emergency room to make ends meet.

I made an appointment with my banker. I was making money, and my credit was good, so I was confident that she would loan me the money to begin my aesthetic medical clinic.

I also knew that I would need to contribute some money to open my clinic. I was paying a heavy student loan debt, so I was not able to save a lot of money yet, but I had some amassed. I needed help acquiring more money, though, so I called a dear friend from whom I had borrowed money in the past, which I paid back on time and with interest.

I went to see her and explained my plan and that I had to get out of my current employment situation as soon as possible. She listened intently and agreed to make me a short-term loan to give me the amount I needed to show the bank.

I went back to my banker, deposited my money, and signed all the paperwork that I needed to begin. I did not tell her that I was going to quit my current job, work at my clinic, and moonlight in the emergency room at night.

I purchased the necessary equipment and leased a nice 900-square-foot retail space in the richest part of Oklahoma City. (Oklahoma City and Oklahoma in general have a lot of people with money.) I wanted to set up my practice in Nichols Hills.

I met with the owner of the complex, and we went over the improvements I would need to make to create four exam rooms, a waiting room, a small office, and one bathroom.

I hired the interior decorator I had used to furnish my house a few years before. She was very talented and helped me come up with my color palette and other design choices. I explained how beautiful Joan's clinic was and that I wanted mine to be as elegant as possible, but I was on a budget. The decorator took the reins on that project and set about making draperies and purchasing the furniture.

I picked out the medical equipment. I had ordered the lasers a few weeks before and stored them in my garage. I then had a trainer come again and teach me how to operate them. I learned laser hair removal, laser skin rejuvenation, and vein care.

Victoria Johnson, M.D.

so knew that I would need to contribute some money to
clinic. I was paying a heavy student loan debt, so I was not
ave a lot of money yet, but I had some amassed. I needed
iring more money, though, so I called a dear friend from
ad borrowed money in the past, which I paid back on time
interest.

ent to see her and explained my plan and that I had to get
y current employment situation as soon as possible. She lis-
ently and agreed to make me a short-term loan to give me
nt I needed to show the bank.

nt back to my banker, deposited my money, and signed all
rwork that I needed to begin. I did not tell her that I was
quit my current job, work at my clinic, and moonlight in
gency room at night.

urchased the necessary equipment and leased a nice
re-foot retail space in the richest part of Oklahoma City.
na City and Oklahoma in general have a lot of people with
wanted to set up my practice in Nichols Hills.

et with the owner of the complex, and we went over the
ments I would need to make to create four exam rooms, a
om, a small office, and one bathroom.

ed the interior decorator I had used to furnish my house a
before. She was very talented and helped me come up with
palette and other design choices. I explained how beautiful
ic was and that I wanted mine to be as elegant as possible,
on a budget. The decorator took the reins on that project
out making draperies and purchasing the furniture.

ked out the medical equipment. I had ordered the lasers a
before and stored them in my garage. I then had a trainer
in and teach me how to operate them. I learned laser hair
aser skin rejuvenation, and vein care.

Me, being silly

Me, at about 27

Just beginning my medical practice

Early morning pool work-outs

From Trophy Wife to Cosmetic

She had long been interested in having
cose and spider veins. She had partnered wi
they opened their own place. She also had
doing Botox and wrinkle fillers, among oth

I visited her one day at her clinic and
beauty of the place. It was so elegant yet p
vide me with some treatments. She is a ve

I got to thinking, if Joan could mak
career, then so could I.

I began researching the aesthetics m
anyone doing much online yet, but I ma
that sold used lasers and that would help
get you trained in different procedures.

I had many conversations with the o
the right direction. He suggested a list of
would be beneficial to my patients and p
medicine is a business too, so the bottom
money.

I spoke with friends and colleagues
my career. As I learned more about the ae
it was just starting to be a viable market a
for new ideas and practices.

I traveled to Los Angeles where I m
an anesthesiologist but had transitioned t
She taught me how to inject Botox and v
trained me on a few laser procedures.

I decided that I could make this mc
that I could always moonlight in the em
meet.

I made an appointment with my b
and my credit was good, so I was confid
the money to begin my aesthetic medica

49

I then asked my daughter to come over and let me practice lasering her. She was excited for me and agreed. She had been bothered with spider veins and wanted to begin treating that issue.

I had her on the table and began lasering her legs. I forgot to put numbing cream on her skin before lasering her, and she still, to this day, calls me to task on this issue. I never forgot again.

I then learned permanent makeup tattooing and treated all my friends and their friends. I'm so grateful for their patience with me, and no one got hurt in the meantime, except me. I decided that I should laser myself and instantly burned and scarred my neck in a few places that are still evident today. I never treated myself again.

Everything was coming together; it was time to hand in my resignation. I got up the nerve and wrote a nice letter to the recruiting officer and the clinic manager about my plans to begin my own practice.

Before I delivered my letter, I met with Dr. Storms, who was still in charge of the emergency room staffing. I told him what I was doing and asked if I could work in the emergency room at night until I got on my feet. He agreed, and we worked out a schedule. He apologized for how poorly I had been treated, and he said he wished there was something he could have done about it.

I then had a meeting with the manager and gave her my two weeks' notice. I had stayed a little longer than three years, so I had fulfilled my agreement with the state that I would practice for three years in a small town.

I then met with the recruiting manager who hired me. I gave him notice, and he said I owed the clinic two more years. He had written that stipulation in my employment contract, and I had missed it—and so did my lawyer. He told me that if I quit now, I would owe the hospital $30,000 interest free. I was dumbfounded and furious but didn't show it.

I didn't think I would survive in that environment for two more years. I made it a matter of prayer. I intensely prayed for guidance, and the deep feeling of peace overcame me. I knew from past experiences that when uncertain about a path to take in life, always go the way of peace.

I had another meeting with the recruiter, and we worked out a payment schedule. I didn't have a job yet, but I was out of there. I paid every penny of the $30,000 within the next few months.

I had hired a crew of workmen that were supposed to be putting in the bathroom and cleaning up the clinic space. Because I was working at night, I had not checked on the progress.

I was finally able to drive the hour commute from the hospital to my new clinic, and when I opened the door, to my utter shock, the bathroom was not ready and there was a huge pile of dirt and trash on the floor. My furniture was coming, and I was to open in two days.

I called a couple friends who were very handy and told them of my dilemma. They quickly came to assess the situation. I cleaned up the pile of trash and washed the floors while my friends got the bathroom in order.

My interior designer had the furniture delivered and the draperies hung. I remember hanging the first picture on the wall. It was so elegant. I was nervous, but there I was, in my new clinic.

I had also hired a media company that helped me build a website and design my logo and letterhead. I was so scared. They also purchased some ads in popular local papers.

Everything I was doing was unheard of in Oklahoma City in 2002. Although I was one of the first to open a strictly aesthetic medical clinic, I was ready. My phone, however, was not ringing. When I opened on July 8, 2002, I had only three patients to see, one of whom was a dear friend who spent a bunch of money with me on my first day.

Things were slow at the clinic, and I continued to work as many night shifts as Dr. Storms would allow. Then I would stay at the clinic all day. A couple months went by, and the clinic continued to be slow. It was not bringing in much money.

In the meantime, my friend Joan began advertising on a local radio station. She said it helped her business a lot. So I thought about my target audience. All of this was new to me, so I had to get educated on marketing strategies.

I decided to call KOMA, a local radio station, and try to advertise on the most popular morning show in Oklahoma. Danny Williams had been a disc jockey for that station for many years and had a huge following.

Even though I was working in the emergency room for months, I still was not making my overhead. After four months in business, I had only $4,000 left to my name.

I spoke with the account executive and purchased an ad campaign on Danny's show. Danny was a very flamboyant showman. He had never heard of the procedures I did, but he wanted to meet with me so that he could better understand what he would be promoting.

He came to my office with his hunting dog, and we chatted for a while, becoming fast friends. Danny was a child of the sixties and was just as wild all these years later. He had a gorgeous wife who agreed to allow me to treat her for free so that she could talk the clinic up as well. Maureen and I are still friends over twenty years later.

Danny frequently had me on his show to talk about my clinic, and he did live commercials for me. He would always get my phone number wrong, so he had to repeat my ad over and over. He would say things like, "LaserLight and Dr. Johnson will take years off your life." The result was that I went from barely making a few dollars a month to making thousands of dollars. Month after month my clinic grew, and my finances greatly increased.

I decided that it was time to quit working at the emergency room. I spoke with Dr. Storms and thanked him for helping me get to a place where I was going to be independent.

Now it was just me and building my practice. I arrived at work early and made sure the toilets were cleaned, the floors were washed, and everything was perfect when I opened the doors.

I sat for days with a few curious people coming by to see what I was doing. It was a totally different concept with Botox, laser hair removal, laser wrinkle remover, and wrinkle filler. I was able to treat rosacea (redness in the skin) as well as melasma, which is a difficult condition to treat because several different conditions contribute to it. Sun exposure and exposure to heat really allow the darkness in the face to be evident.

I experimented with different wavelengths of laser energy to see what I could correct or make better, making most of it up. Over time, I became successful in treating many skin conditions. Then the most amazing discovery revealed itself.

As patients came in for new "foreign" treatments, they shared their lives, and I realized why they were in my clinic. They saw me as a physician, and they wanted to be healed or helped with their many emotional and spiritual problems.

I had a talent, though I didn't realize it at first. One after one, patients came and shared their most intimate problems with me. I was honored and tried to hone my listening skills.

I would ask myself as I picked up a patient's chart, "Why are they really here?" It was the most important question to ask myself. I realized that if I was going to help them with their outer appearance, I was going to have to treat their underlying motive to seek my treatments.

Sometimes patients would be blunt and say things like, "My husband left me for another woman," or a male patient might share that he lost his wife of forty years and was feeling lost.

I knew I had to work on myself spiritually and emotionally if I was going to be of the most help, so I put myself in counseling with a wonderful doctor. She helped me with responses and strategies to deal with the various problems people shared with me.

I realized that I was very judgmental and needed to correct that. I wanted to be accepting of all, even if I didn't necessarily understand a patient's problem. I wanted to be empathetic.

I then began reading spiritual books to help me grow as a person. I learned transcendental meditation and began following Dr. David Hawkins, a spiritual teacher. I found his teaching practical and easy to put into effect in my own life, which would extend to being more effective dealing with my patients. I voraciously read and listened to all his teaching, including his last book, *Letting Go: The Pathway of Surrender*. It was the perfect summation of his work and easy to understand. I purchased this book by the dozens and handed them out to patients I was counseling.

I also began scheduling patients who were really struggling with weekly or monthly counseling appointments and didn't charge them. I just loved it. Helping people find hope is a great gift.

I was happy and joyful, watching my practice grow, and I scoured journals and the internet for the latest procedures. I learned many of them, and I added laser liposuction and thread lifts. I purchased more advanced lasers as they became available, mixing and matching lasers, threads, and skin-tightening procedures to come up with my own treatment packages.

I was certainly a pioneer in the aesthetic medicine arena that didn't even exist when I started. It was a fun challenge to see how I could manipulate the laser energies to achieve my desired goal. I studied laser physics and was fascinated, using what I was learning.

It was also clear that I needed help. A friend of mine had a daughter who had had a stroke in her teenage years and was debilitated. She asked me for a job, and I hired her. Ashley is a sweet, loving, hardworking young lady who worked with me for a couple years.

One day, while I was working, the front door opened and in walked a woman with a slight build. I didn't think anything of it. I greeted her, and she promptly showed me her badge. She was an investigator for the medical board.

I was so scared. No one had a clinic quite like mine, and she wanted to ask me some questions. I agreed, of course, as I wondered what I had done.

She wanted to look through some patient charts and make copies of them. My hands were visibly shaking, and she noticed. She reassured me that this was a routine call and that I wasn't in trouble. (I found out later that the medical board had no idea what kind of clinic I was running, and they were getting complaints from other doctors, wondering what I was up to.)

I was very nice and showed her everything I was doing. She came in a few times to ask me questions and make sure all my licenses and qualifications were up-to-date. She would give me suggestions, and I followed them.

She asked how she could get some training in the different treatments that I offered. I shared with her courses she could take—courses that became available long after I began practice.

She shared with me that clinics like mine were popping up all over without the proper training. I helped her understand what I was doing, and we came up with some guidelines that the medical board could use to make sure the other clinics were in line.

It was fun! I met the executive director, and we became close allies. He would call and ask me questions, and I would call him and offer suggestions.

It was a good relationship.

BIRTHDAYS AND BAD LUCK

As of the writing of this book, I have had my practice for over twenty years. In that time, patients have consistently asked me, "Why do I have all these wrinkles?" or "Why do I have this sagging skin?"

Although there are many reasons (smoking, drinking alcohol, and poor nutrition, for example), what they really want is permission to address the various issues, so I always come back with, "Bad luck and birthdays!"

They would also ask me if I thought they were too vain. I told them that I owned the clinic, so I was the one that was vain. Then we would laugh.

Occasionally an irate husband would storm through the door, demanding a refund from us for fraudulent charges on his credit cards. We would try to usher him away from the packed waiting room while we pulled his wife's chart. We were then able to show that the charges were legitimate, and that his wife received the treatments, signed the consents, and signed the charge slip. (Wives would blame the charges on us, saying we overbilled, etc., to avoid their husband's wrath.)

One day, a patient came in with her husband who was apparently an FBI agent. (Why she thought that was relevant, I hadn't a clue.) She began screaming—again in the waiting room—and demanded to see me and to have the charges on her husband's credit cards reversed. We pulled her chart while she continued to scream at us and call us horrible names. It was then that a darling young man stood up and confronted her about her abusive behavior.

She began to scream at him too. I ran to the back office and called the police, whose station was across the street from my office. The police arrived while the woman continued her barrage of insults. She wouldn't pause long enough for us to show her husband that she had purchased and received services for not only her, but for two of her friends as well.

The police officer was polite and escorted the couple outside the clinic. I then saw the officer draw his pistol! Evidently, the FBI husband reached into his coat pocket for his badge and revealed that he had a gun also. They were escorted off the property. She didn't get a refund and would never be a patient again.

I also had many occasions when the wives brought their husbands in, wanting them to look better. It never failed that the husband was handsome and aging gracefully, while the wife looked twenty years older than her age. I never figured out the dynamic there, but it happened many times.

Through the years I have seen the effects of poor self-esteem. Many patients try to do too many procedures until they don't look like themselves. I have counselled many of them, and the underlying issue is poor self-esteem.

I have also had wives come in for help because their husbands told them they were fat and ugly and no one else would want them. Sadly, this was also not an isolated instance.

I've seen women and men dumped by their spouses for younger people—not necessarily more beautiful or handsome—just younger. I've helped many patients go through difficult times like divorce and death.

I had a lovely older woman come see me the other day, and she was an emotional wreck. She sobbed uncontrollably, telling me that she had lost her husband of twenty-five years a few months ago. Then her dog became gravely ill, and she had to put it to sleep, and her father died a few days before this appointment. My heart broke for her as I just held her hand and let her weep. When she had calmed down a bit, I hugged her, got her a copy of *Letting Go*, and sent her flowers. I see her back this next week; hopefully she will feel better.

During another busy day at the clinic, I had a patient wanting to consult about various treatments. She seemed almost frantic to get started with something, and I felt like something else was going on. I asked her about her urgency.

She began to tell me that she had had pneumonia and had been in the hospital for a few months and then ... died.

"You died?"

She went on to tell me that she woke up in the morgue of the hospital in a body bag. She got herself out and walked out of the morgue to the complete shock of the medical staff there. She then pulled her wallet from her purse and retrieved a small piece of paper, which she handed to me.

It was a copy of her death certificate!

She said, "That's why I must get things done that I've put off for years so that I could take care of my family." She said that she hadn't realized how much she had let herself go. She begged for my help, and we formulated a treatment plan that would address the issues she wanted corrected. She has been my patient for many years and is such an inspiration to me.

CRIMINAL NURSE

I have three sisters who are nurses, and two of them came to work for me for varying amounts of time. They were lovely with my patients and hardworking.

My older sister was a nurse practitioner, which was very helpful. Not at that time, you still have to be a dentist, doctor, nurse practitioner or physician's assistant to operate a clinic like mine. Having her there meant that I was able to take time off without having to close the clinic.

She did all the laser treatments and injectables, while I was in surgery from 6 a.m. to 7 p.m., performing liposuction, thread facelifts, and C02 lasering. We worked Monday through Saturday and were booked out for several weeks. The trend was catching on, and the patients became savvier and were looking for my services.

One day, while finishing a day of work, my older sister told me that she had met someone and was moving back to Houston where she had lived previously. Then she just left. I was in a bind and desperate to replace her when one of our representatives for a laser company came to visit me.

She told me that she had a nurse practitioner who knew how to operate the lasers and do the injectables that I offered. She had been working for a plastic surgeon in the area. I agreed to meet her, and we hit it off immediately. I then hired a former patient and friend to run the front desk. Things went well for a while.

Then I noticed that my sales were really suffering on the injectable side of my practice. My cash was stretched, no matter how much money I made with my surgical patients. This went on for a while until I was unable to pay my suppliers, and my accounts were put on hold. I was unable to purchase Botox or any of my fillers.

I turned to my friend Joan again, who at that point had opened a clinic across the street from mine and offered similar treatments. She agreed to let me pay her cash for my supplies until I could get back on my feet.

I didn't know what was going on, and my accountant was getting nervous too. My nurse practitioner and the receptionist became very mean toward me as I began asking for a log of all the products used on a daily basis.

They refused to give me an accounting, and then the receptionist slipped. She said, "I can't believe how many free services you give away."

What did that mean? I wondered and began to press harder for an inventory system and some accounting of where all the product was going.

I was met with harsher pushback. One day I walked into a patient room where the nurse had been injecting and saw a patient hand her cash. Another time, when I told her not to order items that were used in a particular service, she opened her purse and there were two of the $2,000 hand tips.

She just shrugged it off, and I didn't know what to do. I became very scared and miserable. I was losing my practice that had been thriving a short while ago.

I had also begun keeping an inventory of a small number of narcotics for my surgery patients. I was unaware of the inventory controls and paperwork that would track their arrival to and exit from the clinic.

At that time Oklahoma had no way of showing a practitioner what and who were receiving controlled prescriptions. They had just developed the prescription monitoring program, or PMP. It had been developed to allow a provider to sign in and see what activity was happening under their license number.

When I first logged on, I saw many controlled substance prescriptions. I wasn't alarmed because I was performing four to six surgeries a day that required pain or anxiety control.

I then got a call from a DEA agent. The woman was nice and asked if she could have an appointment with me to discuss some issues that concerned them. I agreed, stupidly. I had no idea what was going on or how to deal with the situation.

The day came when not one, but two agents showed up at my office, badges on full display. If you have never had this happen to you, it is a shocker. I felt like I was going to faint.

I ushered them to my office, and they began asking me questions about the narcotics I had stored in my clinic. I showed them where I had them locked up. They then asked for the log I was supposed to have. I didn't know what they were talking about.

They grilled and grilled me about the prescriptions I had written and the lack of documentation that was to have accompanied my storage of controlled substances. They played good cop, bad cop; one was nice and empathetic, and one was an asshole.

After berating me for hours, they finally left, saying they would be back in touch with me. I was so scared and so lost. I had no idea why they were in my clinic.

I had to go visit my CPA in the next days that followed and happened to mention the meeting with the two DEA agents. I told him I didn't know if I was in trouble, and if I was, how much trouble I was in. He told me not to worry and that he would have the appropriate attorney get in touch with me.

I received a call from Mike Joseph, an attorney of great renown in defending physicians in all manner of problems. He said that he would be in my office at 5 p.m. after the clinic closed.

He showed up promptly, and I went through the whole visit with the DEA agents, describing their concerns. He said that he had had this issue with other physicians' offices.

By the time he left, I felt better. The only problem was, I had no money to pay him. I told him that so that he wouldn't do a bunch of work that I couldn't afford. He again told me not to worry and that we would take care of it later.

I slept for the first time in months, though I was utterly miserable. I had no money. I could no longer afford my house. I sold it and moved with my two large parrots and two dachshunds into a small apartment. I apologized to them and told them that when I got out of trouble I would move us to a home that we wouldn't leave for a long time.

The parrots didn't last long at the apartment. The manager said that they had to go because they were too loud. They are loud! I ended up moving them to my office at the clinic for a while.

I just kept praying and asking for help and guidance. After a while, I fell into a deep depression, and it was the only time in my life that I thought about killing myself. I had been in bad emotional spots in my life but not like this.

The humiliation was horrible. I had advertised heavily in my market and am somewhat of a local celebrity. The thought of closing the clinic and trying to find a job was not appealing to me at all. I thought I might have to move to New Orleans with my parents. I had just enough money to be able to move and little else.

I decided to tell a friend who was also a psychiatrist about my thoughts and predicament. He listened with great intent as I explained. We made a pact that I would not kill myself and that I would keep in close contact with him until I got through this.

Thank you, Paul.

In the weeks to come, Mike, my attorney, would call me with the facts of the "case" the DEA had against me. He was negotiating with them on my behalf.

In the meantime, I had called the medical board and asked them to come to the clinic and go through it with a fine-tooth comb to see if there were other infractions that needed to be corrected. I also worked with a company who specialized in bringing medical clinics into compliance with all kinds of rules that I didn't know existed. I was learning a lot.

The days in the clinic went on. The receptionist quit, and so it was just the criminal nurse and I working.

I got a call at some point from my CPA telling me that he was sending over a man who specialized in helping clinics and physicians get back on their feet.

In came Bob! He wore a black suit and had jet-black hair, reminding me of Johnny Cash. He was a force to be reckoned with.

I introduced him to the criminal and told her that I had hired Bob to go through the clinic's procedures, etc. and figure out what was going on. The criminal begged me not to hire him. I hired him anyway. He told me his monthly fee. I told him that if he could find that money in the clinic, he could have it. So Bob began to look at inventory and cash flow.

The next Sunday, I got a call from the criminal. She laughed as she told me she quit! Wow! OK, so now it was down to me working at the clinic.

I went to work! Just like in the beginning, but this time I asked my sister to help me. I had some other dear friends that jumped in and learned how to operate the lasers and help me with the injectables. It was very uplifting!

Day in and day out, I treated my patients. My cash flow improved dramatically. The criminal had been taking cash for the injectables and procedures and putting it in her pocket. Then I found out she was sending my surgery patients to a local plastic surgeon, who—it was rumored—was having an affair with her.

While treating patients, I noticed that there were notes that the patients had received controlled substances. The amounts were put into the log so the inventory would balance. One by one, I asked them if they received these drugs, and one by one, they said no.

Hmm! She was stealing the controlled substances but had documented them in the patient charts and controlled substance inventory log.

I then began studying my physician's monitoring program list of what prescriptions were written under my license. This was the first time that this program was implemented. Before this you didn't know what was being prescribed under your name.

I was shocked. I printed out the list and began pulling charts of the patients for whom prescriptions had been filled. There were hundreds of prescriptions. As I studied the list, I noticed the names of the criminal's sorority friends. Two of them had repeatedly filled prescriptions "written by me" for forms of speed and sedatives. They filled them at the same pharmacy week after week.

I called the pharmacist and spoke with a woman who listened to my story. She told me that she was about to call me because these two women were filling the same prescriptions weekly, and the pharmacists were suspicious.

I told her that the two women were not patients of mine, and I had no charts for them. I told her that they were friends of my last nurse practitioner. The criminal.

As we were speaking, the pharmacist said, "Wait! One of the women is here to fill a prescription."

She then left the line for a few moments, and when she came back on, she wanted to confirm that I had not written the prescriptions for controlled substances. I again told her that I had not. She then called the police while I was still on the line with her.

The police responded fast and quickly arrested the woman with the forged prescriptions. The woman was a prominent banker in the area, and now she was in the back of a police car. The police officer asked if he could come visit with me about this issue. I agreed, and he met me at my office.

He and his partner had also gone through my log on prescriptions under my name and noticed many other discrepancies. They noticed that I was checking this list at all hours of the day and night to see who else was writing prescriptions. They asked me why I was looking up different names. I told them that I was trying to see if anyone else was in cahoots with the criminal.

I was able to compose a list of prescriptions that had been forged and a list of missing medications that were documented in patient charts that my patients had not received. My lawyer was going to give this information to the district attorney.

I then made an appointment with the nursing board with my lawyer. I had all the entries in the narcotics logs and the notations in patient charts who denied receiving any medications. They said they would take it from there.

My attorney and I also met with the district attorney who issued a warrant for her arrest. I wish I could have seen that.

She quickly hired a criminal defense attorney who bailed her out of jail. She eventually went to trial and received ten years of "hard" probation. I didn't know there were different kinds.

She also lost her nursing license for a period of years, had to go to mandatory rehabilitation for drug abuse, and was forced to attend weekly meetings. She also incurred a large fine.

During this process, I realized that even though I had done nothing wrong (except in my documentation), I was the first person who had been investigated. I endured hours of grilling by the criminal's attorney, trying to make something up that I had done. I had many interviews with other agencies, all of whom found nothing except my lack of documentation.

Oh, well. I didn't do anything wrong except I owned a clinic that allowed a criminal to operate freely, out of my ignorance or whatever you want to call it.

I quickly corrected my deficiencies with the help of the medical board and consultants. I was feeling better, and my business once again prospered.

A few weeks went by, and my lawyer called and said that the government wanted $300,000 to settle this case. I told him that I would deliver the keys of the clinic to them because I was still struggling to get back on my feet.

My attorney said the DEA agents wanted to make an example of me. I said that was fine, but I didn't have that kind of money.

Another week went by, and I received another call from my lawyer informing me that they would settle with me for $60,000. My attorney told me to take the deal. I was allowed three years to pay the sum without interest. I agreed, not knowing how I was going to get another $60,000.

I ended up calling the person that oversaw the program and asked if I could make monthly payments. I figured I had a better chance at small payments. She agreed and altered my agreement so that I only paid a small sum each month until the balance was paid.

I had been cut off by all my suppliers, and the television stations—all except one—wouldn't let me air my commercials without paying off the balance I owed them. The one station that allowed me to continue was one that I had been with for years, and I always paid my bill. He told me that if I would begin paying on the balance and for the commercials that would air, he would allow me to advertise with them.

Thank you, Wes!

I then got a call from the president of a large television station where I had been successful with advertising. He asked how his competitor station let me run on their station. I told him the arrangement that I had with the station, and he agreed to allow me to do the same with his station. That helped grow my business back faster.

Thank you, Brent!

In the meantime, before I knew why I was unable to pay my bills, my dear friend Joan allowed me to pay her for supplies I needed until I could get back in good graces with all my suppliers.

Thank you again, Joan!

I focused on my business and how I could expand it. I learned the latest thread facelift and laser liposuction, as well as traditional liposuction. I wanted to purchase the liposuction machines but was told that the FDA would not let me purchase them until they knew that I was proficient in them.

I practiced and practiced different techniques. The FDA sent a nurse trainer to observe me perform several lipo procedures. He was impressed and asked if I wanted to teach the technique. I thanked him and just asked him to sign off so that I might purchase the machines.

I got approved!

By the time I finished doing liposuction, I had performed over 3,000 procedures. What you don't realize about the medicine I was practicing is that it is physically demanding. My hands, neck, and feet were suffering when I made the choice to no longer offer surgical liposuction procedures.

I did, however, begin doing fat reduction surgeries with lasers, which is much less demanding. I also can train a staff member to perform the procedures.

TO BUILD OR NOT TO BUILD?

I practiced at the same location for thirteen years, renting my space, and over time I acquired the space next door to handle more patients.

I used the same interior designer that had decorated my original office space, and she did an amazing job. My clinic was beautiful.

I received a letter from a group that had purchased the plaza where my clinic was located. They informed me that they would not be renewing my lease at the end of the year. They stated that they wanted only retail stores and not a medical clinic.

I was stunned. I called the property manager and asked him what the problem was. He said the new owner wanted to put big retailers in the plaza, not small boutiques.

I said, "That will never sell in this plaza or neighborhood." He said that he knew that, but he was just the property manager and there was nothing that could be done. I had six months to be out of my rental units.

On the verge of panic, I quickly called my longtime boyfriend (who is now my husband) and told him my predicament. He was so kind and patient with me through the years, and this was another time he jumped in and helped me brainstorm my next moves.

We sat for many hours looking at my financial situation and the logistics of finding another place to rent. Night after night we scoured the city and neighborhoods I thought would be an appropriate location for my clinic. Night after night we failed to be satisfied with places to rent.

I pray constantly most days, and this was no different. I simply had to have an answer on what to do.

It never dawned on me that I should build my own building, though Al, my husband, and Bob, my manager, discussed the situation ad nauseum.

Then one day as Bob and I were having lunch, we were both looking at my financial condition and we said at the same time, "Let's build!"

It felt as if the pieces of a puzzle were falling into place, and I was overcome with peace, the peace that only God can bestow.

Now the hunt was on for a piece of land. That ended up being easy as we drove around looking for a place to build.

I had lived in my house for several years, and there were many office parks close by that were very nice. I thought that surely one of these would work. It wasn't long before I found an office park three miles from my home in a very affluent area. I met with the builder to discuss the process and finances.

I then called the loan officer at the bank where I had been a customer for over fifteen years. I had recently paid off all my loans with them and finally had a cash reserve. I told him that I wanted to purchase a piece of land and build a building. I asked if he would loan me the money.

He asked me to send over my current financials. I did, and they looked good.

He called me a few days later and told me that his bank no longer wanted to do business with me. He told me confidentially that someone high up in the bank had blackballed me.

I was struck with fear. I had been working so hard to recover financially and had been successful. He wouldn't tell me who it was, but I was finished at that bank. (Many years later I found out who had done this to me at the bank and why.)

I called my longtime CPA and told him what the bank had told me. I asked him for help locating a banker that would suit my needs.

Not long after my conversation with Bo, my CPA, I received a call from Shannan, a banker at a bank not far from my clinic. We made an appointment for her to come to my clinic and go over my needs. When she did, we hit it off immediately. She is a vibrant, charismatic young woman.

I laid out where I wanted to purchase land and build a clinic. She was familiar with the area and builder. My CPA had already gotten her up to speed with my financials, and she came prepared. She had the paperwork to transfer my bank accounts to her bank and establish a line of credit.

I was so impressed by her forethought and felt taken care of. I could sleep again.

The builder was a very knowledgeable man who had built several buildings in the office park where I wanted to build. My real estate agent helped me buy the land, and I hired an architect.

I had been working with a feng shui expert for a few years. He also had many years of experience designing and building buildings. He sat down with the architect and made sure the clinic was comfortable for me and my patients. He changed the locations of walls and various other structural elements until he felt that the flow of people through the clinic was correct.

I had only four months before I had to move, so the pressure was on. The builder felt confident that he could get it done, but I had to keep his design that the city planners had already approved. He would just have to get the ground floor designs approved.

That was the longest part of the building process, waiting for approvals from various government departments. The builder knew his way through the process, though, so there were fewer hiccups. We were also blessed with few rain days, which would have delayed the process further.

In the meantime, I worked with my staff as usual, taking care of patients and planning the move. The trickiest part was moving the lasers. I had several different types of lasers, some more delicate than others. I finally decided to move them myself. I would rent a van and carefully handle the job.

My previous interior designer retired, and I was on the lookout for a new one. One of my patients was a locally renowned designer, so I called her. We made an appointment to meet.

Barbara is a few years older than me and is always impeccable in her attire and appearance. She also has a fun personality. We got along immediately.

I explained my vision for the new clinic, telling her that I wanted it to look like an expensive French hotel. That was fitting with my New Orleans upbringing and my favorite style. I wanted golds, greens, and blues, along with gorgeous chandeliers and lovely furnishings.

She worked with the architects and Randy, my fen shui expert, making sure the energy flow and the flow of people through the building were easy and stress-free.

I spent hours with her picking out furniture and fabrics. I knew that she had worked with clients who built elaborate million-dollar homes. That wasn't me. I gave her my budget, thinking that she would balk and tell me that it wasn't enough. She didn't. She said that it might have to look expensive, but it wasn't going to be expensive.

At my last location I had only four small patient rooms, the lobby, the bathroom, and an office in a 1,300-square-foot space. It was tight. I outgrew it years before, but I didn't realize I needed more room to grow. My new clinic was 6,500 square feet. A whopping 3,200 square feet were downstairs, accessible to patients and staff. I built nine patient rooms, a large office space, a finance office, and my office.

The space was circular so that if you kept moving forward, you would end up at the beginning and end of the space. The hallways were widened so that two people could walk side by side down the halls with plenty of space between them. The front doors were huge so that no one had to run into another person whether entering or leaving the clinic. The back hallway was long, and I had many nightmares about how I would fill all that space and walk up and down it every day.

The building process went along quickly. My builder was very proficient at his job, but he was a difficult person. He fought my staff and me about wanting to hang chandeliers instead of boxed fluorescent lighting. He would sneak in industrial lighting, and he wanted to put a steel water fountain in the lobby. He wasn't understanding the look I was going for.

He also built a bedroom and bathroom with a complete kitchen in case I wanted to live there even though my house was three miles away. He also hung large televisions everywhere. He wouldn't listen, so I just quickly changed out his abominations to my pretty things.

The builder also employed his ex-wife, Janet, who was hardworking. She was an older woman who drove a beat-up truck. I learned later that she lived with the builder, who almost constantly berated and belittled her in front of my staff. On several occasions my staff members confronted him and took Janet out of the situation. I never witnessed this, but all my employees complained about it.

On one occasion, Jessica, my right-hand person, told me about a scene where she was screaming and yelling to get the builder away from Janet. She told me that something had to be done to help Janet escape. Through this building process we fell in love with Janet. She was so smart and fun. I decided to offer her a job.

I sat her down and asked her if she wanted to be my personal assistant. I told her that I would purchase her a new truck and rent her an apartment. She seemed skeptical and hesitant. I reassured her that the job was more secure than her current one and that we would take care of her. She told me that she needed to decide what to do for her aging dog, and she also said that she could stay with her longtime friend. She did agree to accept a new truck.

I gave her a copy of *Letting Go* by Dr. Hawkins. As I mentioned earlier, I have given this book out daily for many years. Sometimes people who read it thank me for it.

Janet read the whole thing in just a few days. She had questions about Dr. Hawkins's work and how she could apply his principles in her life.

She finally had the courage to tell the builder that she was moving out and going to work for me. He was livid. He said that that book had messed her up. She said no, it hadn't. "Now I know I don't have to take your abuse," she told him, "and I can have a better job and a better life."

She moved in with her friend and has worked with me for eight years at the writing of this book. She is my assistant, but mostly she is my best friend.

She had an impoverished life, but she was very smart and a wonderful artist in many medias. She could now live in peace. She was smiling all the time, and I could feel a lightness in her, whereas before there was only heaviness.

The time to move in was quickly approaching, but it wasn't in time for my deadline with my current lease to end. I called the property manager and told him that I needed two more months (at the most) to move. I was worried that he wouldn't approve it, but he did.

He told me to just keep paying the rent and send him the keys when I was moved out. Despite my constant worrying, everything continued to work out just fine. God is in control, not Victoria. It is hard for me at times to let go and let God navigate life for me. I was learning that lesson again.

It was time to do a final walk-through at my new clinic. I was shaking. I had watched the painting, and the installation of the flooring, and the hanging of the wallpaper, but now I would see the final product.

The exterior of the clinic is beautiful, and the gardens are immaculate. I opened the front doors and audibly gasped.

It was more wonderful than I had imagined. My designer, Barbara, had enormous French chandeliers hung in the lobby. She had had a fantastic sign hung behind the large front desk. Underneath that sign she had hung champagne-colored wallpaper and champagne-colored glass beads covering the paper. It was breathtaking.

Every room I entered was equally lovely. I finally went to look at my office and stood speechless. It was amazing too. Barbara had created the look and feel of a luxury French hotel in my clinic, and she stayed within my budget!

Thank you, Barbara!

October was almost over, and the weather was changing. Halloween fell on a Friday, and we decided to move the clinic that night.

We frantically packed everything into boxes and loaded the lasers and other equipment into a small van. We worked deep into the night and all weekend too. We were making good progress, and I could see that we would be ready to open at 9:00 a.m. the following Monday.

For the thirteen years that I was in my last clinic, I opened and closed the clinic. Each time I put the key in the lock, I asked myself, *When will I do this for the last time?*

I went to the old clinic after everything had been removed and just sat on the floor and reminisced about the many good and bad times that I had there. I sobbed for a while as I cleaned the bathroom and washed the floors for the last time. I washed all the windows. I wanted to honor the space for being so good to me through the years.

My husband-to-be knew what I was doing, and he decided that it wasn't a good idea for me to spend much time in this endeavor. He called me and told me to wrap it up. We were meeting friends to celebrate, and he was coming to get me in a few minutes.

Suddenly snapped out of the past, I realized that I had a future to create in my new space. I turned off the lights as tears poured from my eyes. I thanked God for all his help through the years, placed the key in the lock, and turned it.

I had a sudden rush of peace and a feeling of hope and joy! The past was over. I had to move on.

We had a lovely dinner celebration with friends, and I got to bed early. I slept like a baby.

LASERLIGHT SKIN CLINIC
15316 N May Avenue
Edmond, Oklahoma 73013

It was time to open for the first time in the new building. I had spent a lot of time with Randy, working on the energy flow of the clinic, as well as the experience that the patients and staff would have. I had a special ornate table placed in the lobby that held a glass vessel that dispensed "spa water." (It was a pitcher of water with various fruits in it.) The goal was to have elegant refreshments.

I also remembered special treats that I received as a child from different stores. I remembered trips to the bank with my mother and the tellers handing the kids in the vehicle different flavored lollipops. I loved it.

I decided that LaserLight would have a signature candy—milk chocolate and dark chocolate Hershey's kisses. I ordered them so that the wrappings matched the current season or holiday. Patients and their kids went straight to them upon entering the clinic, and they have now become a staple.

Through the years we noticed that patients were more irritable around 3 p.m. and less tolerant of having to wait if we were running behind with their appointment times. In the old clinic we had a coffee station, brewing fresh pots all day long. It then dawned on us that after consuming a big cup of coffee as they waited made patients crankier. They were getting too much caffeine and their blood sugar was falling, making them feel irritated. That realization led us to the idea of the spa water plus the candy. It worked like a charm, and the afternoons were much more enjoyable for all involved.

Next, I decided that I wanted special, unique touches that made the patients and staff feel pampered. I worked with a fabulous local florist, hiring him to deliver arrangements of fresh flowers every Monday morning. There are flowers everywhere, even in the bathrooms.

Randall Marsh is so talented. None of his arrangements are ordinary. He uses flowers I could never name, but we all waited excitedly every Monday morning for our daily Starbucks order and Randall's fabulous floral arrangements.

I continued to be the only injector of wrinkle filler and Botox. I also operated the deeper lasers, not wanting to let go of control. I wouldn't let myself travel very much, and when I did, I was only gone for a few days at a time.

I needed to have another physician that would cover the clinic when I was gone. Byron Carpenter was a longtime friend and classmate from medical school, and he jumped at the chance to supervise my staff in my absence. I hired him.

As a seasoned physician, he was very competent and good with my staff, and he was able to handle difficult patients—mainly patients who wanted narcotics or controlled substances for minor procedures or someone who just wanted to get treatments for free.

Byron worked with me for over ten years, and then one day he called me just to chat. In all the time I had known him, we had never done that. I was surprised, but we had a nice visit. He told me that he especially wanted me to hire one of his nurse practitioners, Diane.

She had already filled in for me from time to time when I was sick, etc., and she had been injecting for as long as I had been doing it. We were contemporaries. She lived on a farm forty-five minutes outside Oklahoma City. She is a really a neat person, and over the years we became dear friends.

I listened for about thirty minutes to whatever Byron wanted to talk about, though it was an odd conversation. He was to cover the clinic in the coming week, and I looked forward to speaking with him again.

In the ten years I had known Byron, he almost never cashed his checks. I had to nag him to cash them, and sometimes he wouldn't cash them for six months or more.

He came the next week after our phone call and worked. I left his check on the desk. He always wrote me a kind note at the end of his workday, and this time the note was lengthier, going on and on about life, etc. Again, I thought his behavior odd.

The next day when I was balancing my checkbook, I noticed that he had cashed his check. Wow! More unusual behavior.

The next evening Diane called and asked me if I had heard about Dr. Carpenter. "No," I said. "Why?"

She said that he had shot his best friend and then himself.

I was in shock! What on earth was going on with him?

I was incredibly sad and disturbed for a while. Byron was such a special, caring, fun guy.

Thank you, Byron, for being in my life.

Diane then began working for me on Mondays and Fridays. My hands were bothering me, and the arthritis in my feet was getting worse. The handwriting was on the wall, so to speak. I could no longer do all the procedures by myself.

It was hard to give up control, especially with all that the criminal nurse put me through. My husband convinced me that Diane was not like that and that I should trust her to care for my patients. I decided to try it, and it has worked out great.

At first, when patients only wanted to book with Diane, my feelings were hurt, but my husband quickly pointed out that this was a good thing. It meant I could let go. So I started reading *Letting Go* again. I have read or listened to that book at least a hundred times and always find something else that helps me.

My husband and I started taking a few longer trips as I slowly adapted to not having to work five days a week. My arthritis pain was getting better too.

THE CLINIC: A PLACE OF HEALING!

I was really focused on the patients and staff experience. I am a medical doctor and healer and want that to be evident through the love I try to create in the clinic.

I studied Dr. Hawkins's work and meditated and prayed that the very building would possess a healing aura. It did. Patients and staff were drawn to me, wanting help, understanding, and hope.

Yes, I have an aesthetic medical clinic, treating cosmetic problems, but it was becoming much more by design. Each time I picked up a chart, I asked the Lord how I could help this patient. I usually had a flash of understanding into the real reason the patient had come to the clinic. The reasons were varied, but they needed care and understanding. I was becoming a particularly good listener and was usually able to feel what the patient needed. (I know it sounds kind of weird, but it has been a great gift that I use when treating a patient or staff member.)

One patient comes to mind. A beautiful woman in her mid-sixties, she was well dressed and appeared very confident. When I first encountered her, I reviewed the list of medicines she was taking. (I routinely do this, looking for a clue as to what might be troubling the patient.)

She was on several psychiatric medications for bipolar disorder and antipsychotics. I was intrigued. I learned long ago that no matter what you have experienced encountering patients, you can still be surprised.

I picked up the chart and entered the room. I learned in medical school that you want to sit at eye level or below with a patient. You also want to be positioned in such a way that you and the patient could easily exit the room if either felt trapped or threatened. I also learned that if I were to become overwhelmed and wanted to keep my composure as patients told me horrific things, I would grip the edge of my stool to keep myself from falling off. I was glad that for this encounter I was close to the door.

The patient was sitting comfortably in one of the chairs, and I introduced myself and took a seat on my stool. I asked her what had brought her to the clinic.

She began to speak, and it was quickly clear that the patient was using words out of place. Nothing she said made any sense. In medical school we called this "word salad." It's when a patient just begins speaking gibberish.

Though I was a little alarmed because I had not seen this since my psychiatric rotation in medical school, I did not feel threatened. I just listened to her. She was very expressive and was sure that I was following her conversation. She went on and on, and I let her.

After some time, I did interrupt her. When I did, she seemed to shift inside, as if she realized what she was doing. She quickly pulled herself together and began speaking clearly and understandably. She explained that she wanted help to improve her appearance so that she could feel more confident.

She told me that she had been married for many years but that her husband recently divorced her. She also told me that she had children who would no longer speak to her. She broke down in tears and proceeded to go in and out of garbled speech until she finished describing her life situation.

I thought to myself, *She really needs to see her psychiatrist, not me.*

She insisted on obtaining a treatment plan that would include the issues that were bothering her. I did so, and we produced a plan. I saw this patient at least monthly (if not more) for over fifteen years.

Sometimes when she came in she was coherent and able to carry on a conversation that I could understand. Sometimes she just rambled. I never felt threatened. I had learned that she had no one in the world except a little dog that she adored and the staff and myself. I felt honored to take care of her aesthetic needs.

I did reiterate to the patient that I was not a psychiatrist and was unable to help her with her psychiatric needs. She hated psychiatrists and said that she only wanted to see me. Again, I told the patient that she was going to have to see a psychiatrist who could manage her medication. She did find one finally.

Sometimes a month or two would go by, and I would not see her. She would tell me that she had an "episode" and was admitted to the local psychiatric hospital. I felt so bad for her because she was so alone, but there was only so much I could do.

So I decided that my staff and I would just let her come in and visit whenever she wanted. I think it gave her a sense of "family," but I do not know for sure. I do know that we all looked forward to her visits.

She began bringing in cookies and sandwiches, which was a big hit with my staff.

She explained that she always wanted to be a counselor. We all thought that was a great idea and encouraged her to enroll in school. I do not think that any of us thought that she would do it, but she did! She showed up for an appointment immensely proud of herself. She had enrolled in the local college to become a licensed therapist.

It was impressive to see her shine. She then proceeded to work extremely hard through her coursework. She was surprised to discover that she was smart too. She whizzed through the material and made a group of friends, some of whom were my patients.

They gave me updates on her. They realized that she was not a well person in the ordinary sense, but they loved her and helped her become successful in school.

There came a time when I did not see my patient for a few months, which alarmed me. She then appeared one Friday afternoon and explained that she had been hospitalized again at the psychiatric hospital. I tried to comfort her, but something was different. I could not put my finger on it.

I then did not hear from her again for a few weeks. I got a phone call from one of her friends telling me that she was found dead of an overdose. My heart just wept. I loved this woman and was so frustrated that she would not let me help her get better psychiatric care.

I miss her to this day! Years ago she gave me a pair of earrings that matched a pair that she had. I still have them.

TRANSGENDER

Over the years, I became involved with many different groups because I wanted my clinic to be inclusive, no matter a patient's ethnicity or personal life choices.

I had been involved in the gay community and had many gay friends. A few of them worked in mental health, and I routinely asked them to come in and speak with my staff because we encountered demanding situations when dealing with patients that were struggling with their identity or personal problems. We were unsure how to manage these patients.

My gay friends looked over our paperwork to see if anything was offensive and helped my staff understand how to deal with certain situations. It was an invaluable tool and I thank these people for helping us better understand.

Then one day at work, I saw that a longtime patient had an appointment. He was a ruggedly handsome man and very charming. He and his wife had been seeing me for several years, and I was glad he was on the books. He and his wife traveled extensively and were always fun to talk to.

This appointment was different and left me baffled for a long time.

I entered the room as usual, and we greeted each other warmly. He then told me that he was going to become a woman. He went on to tell me about all the surgeries he had scheduled to change his anatomy.

Again, I held my stool tightly as I tried to force the shock from my body. I wanted to be a professional physician, so I gathered myself up and began to acknowledge what he was saying. He had such an engaging personality, and I genuinely cared for him. I wanted to be happy for him as it was obviously important for him to tell me of his plans. I was just so shocked.

I faked it! I had never heard of this idea or these procedures, and I never thought he was unhappy with himself.

I pushed myself to ask about all the particulars of his upcoming procedures. He was very wealthy, so he had the best surgeons at his disposal. I tried to follow everything he was telling me without falling off my stool.

We planned the treatments that I would do for him, and he scheduled his next appointment. With that done, I ran to my office.

I was so scared for my patient and appalled at my ignorance. I felt blindsided. I needed help and information. I turned to one of my gay friends and explained what I had encountered. She told me not to worry. She said would bring a friend with her who could help explain. My friend Kris made an appointment to bring her friend Paula, formerly Paul, in to help me and my staff with these new developments.

The morning came when Kris and Paula came to the clinic to talk with me and my staff. We all gathered in the head office to listen to their presentation. Paula was introduced to us. She had been an Oklahoma City police officer for many years and a highly decorated military officer. She was over six feet tall and of large stature. She wore makeup and a nice dress, and she was well-spoken.

She was so gracious and allowed us to ask our questions without losing her cool. We just needed information so that we could help this segment of our patient population. The information was shocking and foreign.

She explained that she had always felt at odds with her body and the way that she felt inside. She had been married to a woman and had children, but never felt that her body matched her feelings of femininity that she felt was her true self. She decided long ago that, when she was financially able, she would begin the transformation process, which she did.

Then she explained that her wife left her, but she had met another woman when she was a man with whom she had fallen in love. The woman was a lesbian. I had a problem with this part and still do not understand. ... *You are a man who had been married to a woman. You had a gender-affirming procedure and wanted to date another woman who is a lesbian. So now you are a lesbian too? Why was it not enough to be a man with a woman, rather than change your anatomy to become a woman to be with another woman? What is that?*

I adore Paula and her wife, and I guess I will never understand. My staff were baffled too, and we just decided that it was not necessary for us to understand. However, it was necessary to be kind and loving and to do an excellent job caring for and treating these patients just as we did any other.

Many years have passed since this first encounter, and we have many transgender patients, each with their own challenges. Some had wild emotional swings from the hormone manipulation that they were undergoing and were not always stable or kind. We were the victims of many "raging" patients that were undergoing their transformation. Over time, we got better at treating them and had to set up definite boundaries while they went through the process of becoming physically a man or a woman.

I didn't understand why most of the patients that wanted to become female were large masculine men. It did not make sense. They were not going to fool anyone. You cannot make large male hands feminine.

That is the point! I realized. They were not fooling themselves anymore. It did not matter what other people thought. They had to be true to themselves.

Now, I finally understand.

CHRISTMAS PARTIES!

I love Christmas!

Each year as the holiday season approaches, my assistant, Janet, and I get into gear planning our Christmas party. We always have it at a nearby steak house that my husband and I have frequented for years. The owner and staff are so awesome. They know that we will be loud and raucous, so they give us a private dining room that can be sealed off from the rest of the restaurant. We also come in at 5 p.m. after they first open, hoping that it will not be too crowded.

Janet plans and executes the decorating of the room. She works so hard, producing new decorating schemes that are always over the top! She works for weeks ahead of time and then arranges the delivery of the decorations and other party paraphernalia.

A few months in advance, we brainstorm ideas for gifts to give each staff member. We always want to have some type of functional container (a purse, etc.) in which to place their gifts.

One year, I decided that I needed a couple five-gallon plastic tubs for my garden. I ordered two from Amazon to be delivered to the office. Well, I do not always get my orders correct. It baffled me as to why I couldn't just order two of the buckets and ordered sixteen instead! (Later I would understand exactly why my counts were off—after I had my cataracts removed. My vision was 20/20 and I had no more problems with ordering the wrong quantities. Now what to do with the twenty king-size purple bed covers that I had ordered in my blindness!)

This year, after missing the deadline to return the buckets, I decided we would use them for our container for Christmas. They worked out perfect. We always give each staff member a ham and miscellaneous products that they use during the year at the office. Boxes of Tylenol, ibuprofen, Midol, and Tums were among the usual presents, as well as nail files, socks, and everybody's favorite—ranch dressing! (My whole staff is addicted to it, including myself.)

I then gave everyone their Christmas bonus check and left it as a place card on the table where they sat.

I allowed them to order whatever they wanted from the menu, and we had designated drivers assigned in case someone overindulged. We had the parties on a Friday night so that everyone would be rested for Monday morning.

During the party, we played "LaserLight" trivia. I made up questions about the clinic that no one would have paid attention to, like, "How many stairs are there in the staircase going up to the second floor?" Silliness, but they loved it.

I had a pile of Amazon gift cards that we hung on a Christmas tree. When someone got an answer right—or close to right—they got to pluck a card off the tree. What they did not know was that, at the end of the evening, I picked up everyone's cards and redistributed them so that everyone had the same number of cards.

I wanted everyone to feel special and equal. In an office with more than fifteen employees, there was always going to be drama. My goal was to keep it to a minimum, and I tried to have events such as the Christmas party and daily lunches that helped us bond as colleagues.

Another strategy that I employed to help us bond as a team was weekly meetings held on Wednesday mornings. Wednesdays were a challenge because we had "Walk-in Wednesdays." A patient could walk in without an appointment and receive Botox injections. The patient might have to wait, but the procedure was so quick that they usually did not have to wait long.

It worked out well and helped us gain many new patients. Plus, established patients who hadn't been in the clinic for a while were able to be treated without having to wait six weeks to get an appointment.

Knowing that we would always be tired at the end of the day, I ordered Starbucks coffee and breakfast items for the meeting, which was mostly upbeat. I awarded cash for the most reviews received and number of skin-care items sold.

I purchased a "money gun" and loaded it with small bills. When the winners of various contests were announced, I sprayed their money prize into the air. It was a big hit and always a blast. My CPA would make the necessary adjustments to their paychecks.

Three to four times a year, I also planned pool parties at my home. Janet always invented fun games to play in the pool and would fill the backyard with brightly decorated signs and banners. She blew up about twenty large round colorful floats so that everyone could float around and visit.

We chose teams and played red rover or watermelon roll (where you put a small watermelon on the bottom of the pool and the two teams must roll it from the deep end to the shallow end). They were creative when it came to winning a game.

I had various prizes for each winner, maybe a glass jar filled with dried beans or rice. They opened them quickly, believing that I had placed some money in amongst the various items. Sometimes I did, and sometimes it was just a jar of dried beans. It was always a big hit.

I sometimes grilled steaks and served baked potatoes, a huge salad, and dessert. I wanted them to know that I wanted to take care of them and spoil them.

Other times we had a potluck party. Some came up with elaborate dishes to show off their culinary skills; others who were not so talented brought sodas or chips. We also invited friends of the clinic, my banker, and our suppliers.

Our Thanksgiving party was over the top as well. I always roasted a giant turkey and made giblet gravy and mashed potatoes. Using okra from my summer garden that I had frozen, I fried it up with bacon. Yum!

Some of the girls were particularly good at a special dish. Heather made her jalapeno poppers dish, and Adrienne was charged with making her fantastic mac 'n' cheese!

We extended our lunchtime so that everyone was together at the same time. (Usually, we had two lunchtimes when employees were assigned to take their lunch.) We were so stuffed, but we cheered each other on to work through the afternoon!

I tried daily to keep up the mood in the clinic. I played upbeat dance music in every room so that we "danced" the day away! I jumped in and helped with the laser treatments when the staff got backed up and our schedule was running behind. In turn, they "flipped" my rooms for me, cleaning and putting another patient in my exam room so that I kept on schedule as well.

Over the years, different representatives from various vendors wanted to spend a day with me and watch my operation. I did not mind, but I warned them to wear a good pair of running shoes! I averaged 20,000 steps a day while taking care of patients. They were amazed and very tired at the end of the day!

I have always been blessed with an abundance of energy. God also gave me the ability to stay extremely focused and attentive to my patients' needs. I could pick up on their moods and know if there was a problem I needed to address with them. I would stop in my tracks, pull up my stool, and begin asking them what was wrong. Sometimes it threw off my schedule, but I did not care. This was why I became a physician. I loved taking care of my patients, and they could tell.

MY COFFIN!

One day while seeing patients, I picked up the next patient's chart and began reviewing the information. This patient was new to my practice. She had already been placed in an exam room for me to see her and address her needs.

I opened the door to find an attractive, middle-aged woman sitting comfortably in a chair. I introduced myself, and as I sat down on my stool to begin our conversation, I asked how I could help her. She told me that she would like for her lips to be a little bigger.

This was a common request, so I thought nothing of it. I examined her further and began to get a better feel for what she wanted to achieve. I assured her that I could take care of her and described how the procedure was performed.

As I continued to speak with her, she sighed deeply and told me, "I want to look better in my coffin."

My hands gripped the edges of my stool once again, bracing for the continuation of the story.

She went on to tell me that she had a terminal illness and that there was nothing left to do but wait to die.

I took some deep breaths as she explained that she had a daughter and that a family member would raise her. She went on to tell me about the arrangements that she was making for her funeral.

I could feel her sadness and her resolve. She was almost at peace with it but was struggling to finish tying up loose ends before her demise.

I just sat there in front of her, listening to her story and feeling her pain. Sometimes I don't know why a person comes into the clinic, but this one needed something that I had.

We finished the appointment, and I was determined to have her return for her treatment. She scheduled our next meeting, and I returned to my office. It was hard not to break down in tears for this woman, but I had a clinic to run. I would have to revisit this emotion later.

I saw this patient several times and always made myself available to her so that she could talk about whatever she needed to. She kept returning, wanting some other small treatments, but I knew that she was there for me to care for her at the end of her life.

During one appointment, I noticed a cut on her forehead and inquired about it. She explained that she had fallen and hit her head. She was quite concerned that it would leave a scar. I reassured her that I would take care of it and that my laser treatments would help with scar formation. She seemed relieved.

I saw her many times over the next few months for various things, knowing the visits were for something much deeper. Over time, I felt her anxiety diminish. We joked and laughed at times as I treated her. She was shifting within herself, and I had the sense that she was letting go of the burden of dying. She was such a delight.

The last day I saw her, she was short of breath and told me that she could feel the tumors in her abdomen. She said that she knew the end was near. Her appointment finished, and I walked her to the door. She gave me a big hug, and her face was glowing. She was ready to die.

I never saw her again. She left me with a feeling of peace and relief for her. It was a special relationship. I know that she looked great in her coffin.

YOU NEVER GET OVER IT!

Patients always asked me if I thought they were vain for wanting cosmetic procedures. I always laughed that off, stating I owned the clinic! I also explained to them that if a procedure helped them feel more confident, then that was just fine. I went on to say that my oldest patient was ninety-three!

She came to see me one day accompanied by an aide. She had no family, but this lovely young woman helped her get from one place to another. She explained that she was going to change nursing homes and had some spots on her face that she wanted removed so that she could start dating again! She told me that she learned long ago not to give up on your looks and to do procedures that would help you feel more confident about yourself.

She had been a successful businesswoman throughout her life. Although she was wheelchair-bound now, she was dressed impeccably for each visit, and I always enjoyed my time with her. She asked me about my business, and I asked her to tell me about her business adventures. She was a delight.

She progressed with her treatment plan and had scheduled a follow-up appointment. We took the usual "before" and "after" pictures so that we could make sure that we did a good job for her. I had them printed out and showed them to the patient. She looked great and had not a single spot left on her face. She beamed, seeing the results of her treatments. She shared with me that she was skeptical at first, but after seeing the results, she was pleased.

She told me that she had found a new nursing home and had moved. She also shared with me that she had begun dating a few gentlemen.

I was so happy for her and really enjoyed the spirit of joy that she possessed. She told me, "You never get over wanting to look and feel your best!"

That was the last time I saw her.

TRAPPED!

Over the course of my practice, I have encountered many groups of people. Patients who feel trapped are close to my heart because I was trapped in a bad relationship.

Women and men came in for an appointment because they were unhappy. As I mentioned before, the most valuable thing for me to find out was why a patient was there to see me.

Most often it was women who presented with a certain concern that they would like me to help them with. Their husbands were usually the breadwinners, and they might or might not have had an education, a job, or a skill. This left them vulnerable to being abused. They were trapped in intolerable situations and had no way out.

Many times, my staff and I helped them realize that there was a better way to live, and it often started with a copy of *Letting Go* by David Hawkins, MD. The book gave patients a road map for gaining personal power and helping them find a way out.

One patient who came to see me would just cry. I learned to sit and just be present. I also employed my habit of gently grabbing the edge of my stool. I handed this young lady a box of tissues and waited for her to finish sobbing. She used a copious number of tissues. (I learned to always have a box ready in every room, just in case someone began to cry. It happened a few times a week, and I wanted us to be ready when the time came.)

She took a deep breath and began to explain that she and her husband had been married for many years. They had not been able to have children, but that didn't seem to bother her. She explained that she and her husband had a large boat at a lake north of town and that they would go almost every weekend. They had many friends at the lake, and it was a fun time for them.

On one weekend, her husband decided to go to the lake a few days before she came so that he could make sure some repairs were being done. She packed up and headed to the lake by herself to meet her husband. She got to the dock and greeted their friends as she made her way to their boat. She opened the door to the boat and began to unload groceries and provisions for the weekend, but she kept hearing a noise coming from the master stateroom. She dismissed it a few times as being noise coming from the lake. As the noise persisted, she decided to investigate.

She made her way down the hall to the door of the stateroom and could hear her husband's voice. Not thinking anything of it, she opened the door and was immediately confronted with her husband and another man having anal sex.

She could barely get the words out as she was telling me. My hands were gripping my stool so hard my fingernails hurt.

She said that she didn't say a word to her husband, she was in such a state of shock. She and her husband had a good sex life, and she had no idea that he was interested in men. She backed out of the room and exited the boat, jumped into her car, and sped home. She wouldn't take his phone calls for the next while.

She began sobbing again. She said she had no education and no money of her own and had no idea how she was going to get out of this situation. I let her finish crying and allowed her time to gather herself together. Then I excused myself from the room for a few minutes as I went to my office to get a copy of *Letting Go*.

When I came back to the room, she said that she felt embarrassed that she had shared that experience with me. I told her that it was appropriate for her to feel comfortable telling me this most personal experience. I explained that in my practice, I did a lot of counseling for various issues. I told her that I felt honored that she had told me.

I gave her the book and asked her to promise me that she would read it. She agreed, and I made a follow-up appointment for us to visit again.

Time went by, and I saw her name on my schedule. I was happy that she had scheduled an appointment with me. I picked up her chart and reviewed it as a sick, gut-wrenching feeling brewed inside me. I walked into the room to find my patient dressed nicely and thoroughly composed.

I asked her if she had read the book. She said that she had read it twice and planned to read it again.

I shared with her that I had listened to it or read it at least a hundred times. She believed me, and we shared a moment talking about how the book had helped us see situations and people in a different way. She then brought up the subject of the experience that she had with her husband.

She told me that he finally came home and wanted to talk. He told her that he had a long struggle with his sexuality and was preferring to have sex with men. In the meantime, my patient had been working on herself and her situation. She had found a job at a local dress shop and was enjoying it.

Her husband hated her newfound freedom and began asking her why he could no longer intimidate her. She wouldn't answer.

She then told me that she had always wanted to become a nurse and had a few prerequisite courses in the past that she loved. She had enrolled in pre-nursing school and was excelling at it. She told me that her husband would rage at her when he saw her studying. I shared that my husband had done the same thing to me.

I told her, "You must just keep going forward and ignore whatever he persecutes you with."

She told me that he caught her reading *Letting Go* and screamed that he knew she had been infected with some weird knowledge that allowed her to abandon her husband. He tore the book to pieces and told her that she was forbidden to read that book.

I asked her to excuse me for a moment. I went to my office and retrieved two copies of the book.

When I returned, I told her how proud I was of her and that I knew she had the strength to get herself out of the situation. I then gave her the two books and told her that was just in case another copy was destroyed. She smiled and gave me a big hug.

I have seen her many times over the years, and she did go on to have a successful career in nursing. She divorced her husband and was in a nice relationship with someone new.

I could feel the joy and happiness within her. Yes! There is a way when you cannot see a way. Sometimes you just need some new information and a little support to find your own inner strength. It is there within us all.

WHAT BOTHERS YOU!

I had a new patient encounter scheduled for a routine procedure to help ease the appearance of lines on her face. I came into the room and found a young woman sitting on my exam table, her face completely covered by her long hair. I quickly realized that the hair was a cheap wig, and the patient was wearing it poorly.

I began the interview, as usual, with, "How can I help you today?"

The woman explained that she hated the lines across her forehead. She asked if I thought they were very deep.

I got up from my stool and brushed the hair from her face. She started to knock my hand away, but I told her that it was impossible for me to see her face. She seemed relieved at my answer and allowed me to continue moving her hair away. When I got to a point where I could see her face, I was stunned. This woman was one of the most beautiful women I had seen in my life. I was intrigued.

I handed her a mirror so that she could show me what she was talking about. She began pointing out imaginary lines on her forehead. I learned long ago that it didn't matter what I saw; it was what the patient saw. I had angered patients when I first began my practice.

They would ask me what I would suggest they do to enhance their appearance. I eagerly shared with them various treatments that would benefit them, but some of them stopped me in my tracks, telling me that what I saw didn't bother them at all. Did I not see the tiny brown spot in their hairline (or some other insignificant perceived problem)?

I now just addressed my patients' concerns. In this case there wasn't a line on this woman's face, but she kept pointing them out.

I looked back over her history and noticed that she had been diagnosed with alopecia, a genetic condition in which your hair doesn't grow on your head in various patterns. Sometimes the patient would have patches of hair, and others were almost completely bald.

We discussed options to "correct" the lines on her face, and then I turned to her charts and asked her about the alopecia.

She told me how horrible her hair growth was as she replaced the cheap hair over her beautiful face. I told her that I had helped many alopecia patients over the years. She poked her face out of the hair and was curious.

I asked her if I could see her head without her wig. She agreed, though it took her a few minutes to unpin the wig from her head.

Underneath the wig was a minimal amount of hair loss. I asked her about her husband, and she stated that he was very supportive of her condition.

I spoke with her for a while and told her of a colleague who specialized in covering up patients' thinning hair. I told her that he could make her a hairpiece that would look fantastic. I also told her that it was a shame that she felt so bad about herself that she wore a wig that covered her face. I told her she was beautiful, but no one could see that because she was so covered up. I told her that I had seen thousands of patients, and if I told her she was beautiful, she was!

I left the room to return with a copy of *Letting Go*. I asked her to please read it and go visit my colleague about a wig that would be more appropriate and that would highlight her good looks.

A couple weeks passed, and I noticed that she was on my schedule for a follow-up visit. I was in a hurry, going from room to room, trying to stay on schedule, when I picked up her chart and began to read about our last encounter. I was delighted to see how she was doing. My nurse told me that I was not going to recognize her. I remembered the horrible wig and her frumpy clothes and wondered what she had done.

I entered the room and was blown away at the sight of my patient. She said, "Dr. Johnson, do you remember me?"

"Of course, I do," I said, "but I hardly recognize you."

There sat a gorgeous, smiling young woman wearing a short, cute wig. Her eyes shown bright as she told me about having read and reread that book. She also went to see my colleague who had made her a hairpiece.

She said that after that she began to see her outside beauty, and she was also realizing her inner beauty.

She was well-dressed and sat with her shoulders in perfect posture, radiating confidence. She told me that her marriage had been good, but her husband couldn't make her see her beauty. She then told me that she didn't think that she needed her "wrinkles" treated. We both laughed, and I agreed. There were no wrinkles.

DIFFERENT CULTURES

I have encountered many different ethnic groups in my practice. I was familiar with most of them, but some were a complete surprise.

For a while, women dressed from head to toe in elaborate gowns that covered their whole bodies, including their faces, appeared at the clinic. Some of them even had a sort of metal cage around their eyes and mouths. I wasn't familiar with this dress at the time. The women would be escorted by their husbands, who would only allow me to speak to them, not their wife. I didn't know how to handle this, but I knew what it was like to be a woman who was beaten down.

I decided that these women were my patients and I was going to speak with them. I would ask the husband if the wife could speak English, and most of the time they would say yes. I would then explain to the husband that I had to speak to my patient. Sometimes they objected, and I would explain to them that in this country, I needed to be able to speak to the wife directly because she was my patient.

Sometimes the women were scared and barely said anything. It was difficult to figure out what they wanted from me and how I was going to remain a professional but also empower the wife.

I had several of these consultations, and then one day I noticed that the men were not bringing their wives to me anymore. In my clinic, women were empowered, but not these women.

I then had a group of younger women that would come in as a big group. They tried to overpower my staff and myself, lounging all over the waiting room, and when it was time for their prayers, they would prostrate themselves on the floor and begin screaming in an unfamiliar language.

This scared my staff, so I went out to the lobby and asked the women to leave. I told them we didn't pray that way and that they were scaring my staff and the other patients. They settled down then and scattered their belongings all over the place so that no one else was able to sit. That was when I realized they were loitering to use my Wi-Fi connection.

After that, whenever they came for an appointment, I called my IT person and had him turn off my Wi-Fi while they were in the clinic. That worked!

When I got them alone in an exam room for their laser treatments (usually laser hair removal), they would take off their burkas, sadly revealing that some of them had been savagely beaten by their husbands. I asked them about it, and they said that was their custom while having sex. I asked if they needed help escaping their husbands, and they always said no. "That is just our culture," they told me. Wow!

Another phenomenon was patients coming in for "anal bleaching." My staff and I had no idea what that was. A friend of mine in Los Angeles had a clinic like mine, so I called her and told her about the newest wrinkle in my aesthetic practice. She knew all about it and went on ad nauseum about what it was and how it was treated and the reason patients wanted the procedure.

Evidently, in some cultures it was a status symbol?

OK, well now we knew what it was and a possible motivation for a patient desiring this treatment. (I still don't get that, but that's how it goes. Again, I don't have to understand.)

TRAINER BECKY!

My clinic had been open for a few years when I realized that I wasn't working out much and that I needed help with motivation. I found Becky's ad in the Yellow Pages in 2004, and we have been training together ever since.

She's a few years younger than I am, but we have both been athletes all our lives. Becky was a triathlete, and I had been a long-distance runner, an aerobics instructor, and a long-distance cyclist. Those activities begin to haunt you as you get older. My hips, feet, or hands woke me up many times a week. I didn't think my body would tolerate my previous exercise regimens. Over time, Becky and I realized that swimming would be the best exercise for us.

I had a heater put in the pool in my backyard. Nearly every morning she and I slip into the warm water around six thirty. Somedays we are more energetic than others and put on some dance music, retrieve our noodles, hand weights, and exercise bands, and start moving.

We swim year-round. The lowest temperature that we have swam in was eleven degrees. We swim in the snow, sleet, or rain—if there isn't any lightning. We both have lightning detectors on our phones, but we keep an eye on the radar.

Some mornings we chatter away while our bodies keep time with the beat of the music. I have numerous colorful clay flowerpots surrounding my pool, and Becky and I keep them filled with beautiful vines and flowers. We look for flowers on sale at Lowe's or Home Depot and nurse them to health, babying them in the pots until they are beautiful.

I also have many bird feeders scattered in the trees and on shepherd's hooks. We have a pair of binoculars by the side of the pool along with our phones. Many different species of birds are attracted to the backyard, and we started using the binoculars so that we could look up the various species of birds that we saw.

We both joined social media sites that provided support for birdwatching enthusiasts. We have learned so much about the birds native to our state and when they migrate.

We also noticed that we were attracting hawks to the backyard, so we began to study them as well. We learned about red-tailed hawks, red-shouldered hawks, Mississippi kites, Coopers, and sharp-shinned hawks.

They are quite impressive birds. Many mornings one or more will perch on my fence or roof for a photo op! We whip out our phones to take as many pictures of them as we can and post them on the social media site where other birdwatchers help us identify them.

For many years I have had two parrots, a blue and gold macaw and a rose-breasted cockatoo. They love to talk, and each have a nice vocabulary of about fifty words. There is rarely a quiet moment during the day at my house.

I also have been a gardener since I was a young girl. My mother and grandmother had a large garden, and I loved to help them with it. I remember sitting on my grandmother's porch, shucking peas and chitchatting together.

My mother loved growing roses and lilies, so I learned to do that as well. That was a hobby that my mother and I could talk about when we were unable to talk about anything else.

So I have a large vegetable garden in my backyard as well. Becky and I plan out each year what we should grow, and we compare our crops to the previous years. It's not easy to grow vegetables in Oklahoma. We have frequent droughts, lots of wind, and sporadic freezes and frosts.

Becky and I have learned the hard way not to start your vegetables outside until the second week of May. We even lost a garden one year, planting that late, but usually it works out fine.

We grow several varieties of tomatoes, green and yellow peppers, onions, cucumbers, okra, zucchini, yellow squash, peas, asparagus, broccoli, brussels sprouts, cauliflower, and blackberries. It is fun when the crops begin to produce. My sister Laurie taught me how to can and make pickles, and how to process, dry, or freeze the excess vegetables.

Becky has a small courtyard at her house that she has packed with vegetables as well. We spend hours pruning the vegetables and the plants in the flowerpots while talking about the best ways to feed and take care of our various plants.

We read a lot while swimming. We sit on a small noodle so that our shoulders are under the water, and we kick to the beat of the music.

For many years my husband was the only one to take care of the pool. Sometimes he would forget to add water or to turn something on or off, so the pool would be cold in the mornings. Because of this, Becky and I went to "pool school" while swimming. We wanted to help my husband and have a better chance of the pool heater staying on. It's worked out well.

We joke that instead of swimming or water aerobics, we should call our exercise sessions "pool maintenance, animal husbandry, canning specialists, and exercise nuts."

I keep the pool temperature around ninety degrees, which is perfect for an old, creaky, painful body. It's also amazing what a great workout you can get by swimming.

My yard is surrounded with many old pear, oak, and sycamore trees, which becomes a problem in the fall when the leaves begin to fall. Becky and I love to spend our "exercise" time cleaning the leaves out of the pool. It's a pretty hard task while seated on a noodle, using a long pole with a net on the end, trying to fish leaves out of the deep end.

One weekend, I went out of town, and no one checked on my pool. When I returned, I found that the pool water had turned light brown. The warm water had steeped the leaves that had fallen into the pool and made what we called a "pool tea."

I now have a cover that Becky and I use to cover the pool while we aren't in it. It helps with the leaves, but we have a pair of mallard ducks that love the heated pool as well who just sit right on top of the cover. It doesn't seem to bother them at all.

We use the pool noodles to exercise and do our stretching. Some early mornings, when we were half-asleep, a spider would come marching out of the hole in the noodle and climb onto us, catching us off guard. We hated that, so we began to be meticulous in making sure there were no bugs, especially spiders, inside the noodle. We weren't always successful and would end up with one of them crawling on us. Ugh! There had to be another solution!

We went online and found that we could purchase noodles of various sizes without holes in them! Eureka! The spiders and bugs still float on them, but at least we have a better chance of spotting them before another incident occurs.

As I mentioned, I have large, old trees surrounding my yard. They are also all over the neighborhood. One year we had a deep freeze, and the temperature was below zero for over ten days. Becky and I decided that it was too cold to swim.

It rained and sleeted as well, coating all the trees surrounding me until large branches snapped off, stripping the trees until only large poles were left. It looked as though I were surrounded by a forest of ship masts. I was not convinced they would recover. You could hear the branches popping off the trees all through the night while the wind whipped around. It was heartbreaking to see and hear.

My husband reassured me that he had seen this happen before and that the trees would recover. I was skeptical but saw that after a few years, almost all the trees had regrown their branches and looked the same as they did a few years before.

A few of my friends are avid gardeners as well. My friend Joan is as obsessed with her vegetable gardens as Becky and I are with ours. She began taking online courses and sharing her knowledge with us.

One day, she called and told me that she purchased a particular kind of worm for her garden. I was fascinated and asked her to explain. She told me that we needed to have a worm farm. I had no idea what she was talking about, so I let her explain.

Evidently, you can purchase "red wiggler" worms online and set up your worm farm. She explained how you purchase this plastic worm house that has several shelves that were screens. You place the worms in a nice bed of garden soil on the top shelf and cover them with wet newspapers. You then place their food in one corner. She told me that she fed her worms bread and vegetable scraps. There were some dos and don'ts, but it was straightforward.

The point of all of this is that over time, as you keep your worms warm and fed, they supply their excrement. This waste falls through the screens until it filters its way to the bottom shelf. Their urine also collects in the very bottom tray that has no holes in it.

I was instructed not to use the urine and to discard it. I was to gather the excrement from the shelf and mix it in a five-gallon bucket with distilled water and a small amount of molasses. I was then to place a fish aerator in the bottom and turn it on.

Over the course of the next few days, the organisms that lived in the worm poop multiplied, and I could pour the "worm tea" into another container to water the vegetable garden plants with it. It really did make them grow faster and fatter.

Over the years, I realized that I wasn't willing to go out of town for a long period of time because I would obsess over the health of my worms. Of course, I kept this concern to myself for fear that someone would think I was crazy. In the summer, I worried if the worms were too hot or dry.

I kept my worm farm in my laundry room closet, which was perfect, except for the fact that it was getting messy, and I was worried that my granddaughter would discover them and want to play in the mud. So I placed the farm under a big tree in my backyard where it was shielded from the wind.

They did well until winter set in. Then I brought the worms back in and put them in a large box in my garage where I placed a heating lamp nearby so that the worms wouldn't freeze. They were becoming cumbersome, and I was growing weary of constantly worrying about my worms and if they were happy.

I finally had enough and early one spring day, I called a fellow organic gardener and told her of my worm dilemma. She completely understood and told me that she had built a free-standing, climate-controlled shed where she kept her worms so that she didn't have to worry about them. I felt better that I wasn't the only one who worried about the lives of their worms. I offered her my worms, and she promptly came and picked them up.

She now periodically will give me an update on the worms that I gave her. She also kept bees and tried to convince me to keep bees.

I live in the middle of a city. I don't think beekeeping would be a good idea.

Several years ago, I wanted to grow asparagus. I knew it was a difficult vegetable to grow, but I was up for the challenge. Becky and I began researching how to grow it. We learned that I needed a two-year-old bulb, and that I was to plant it and wait two more years before harvesting it.

I planted the bulbs in a particular place, thinking it was going to be a great spot. A few weeks went by, and then a friend came over to see my garden. (When you find a fellow gardener, it is easy to obsess about gardening.) She was looking at my garden, and we were discussing the varieties of plants that I had.

She came to where the asparagus crowns were placed, and she told me that I had planted my bulbs upside down! I was so embarrassed. The bulbs looked like a space alien, and both ends looked the same to me. So we turned them right side up, which really helped them grow. I was wandering why I didn't have any sprouts or sign of life from the plants.

The asparagus grew slowly over the years, but then after the second year, the sprouts were ready to harvest. We enjoyed the vegetable for several years. Asparagus grows year-round in my area.

One day, I was clearing my garden for the winter vegetables to replace the summer ones and had finished except for trimming the asparagus. I came home from work and noticed that the plants were gone. I couldn't figure out what happened to them.

I then got a call from my yard maintenance man. He was very animated and told me that he knew that I was pulling up my garden and he wanted to help. He told me (much to my shock) that he had tilled up my garden beds and pulled up what he thought was a weed! My asparagus was history.

I didn't tell him what he had done. Instead, I thanked him for so thoroughly maintaining my yard. I did ask him that, from that point on, when he was going to work in my garden beds, I wanted to be present.

I went to the gardening store and purchased more two-year-old asparagus bulbs and made sure that the bulbs were planted correctly. The new plants have never been able to keep up the production that my original ones did. I miss my asparagus.

One bright spring day, my yard maintenance man knocked on my door and told me that he had been chased down the street by a swarm of bees. I was confused as to why this was my problem. He asked me to step outside my front door, so I did and was shocked at what I saw. An enormous group of bees were clinging to the side of my house just outside my front door.

I walked around them and saw that they were going in and out of a tiny pinhole of an opening above my bay window. That window had a decorative copper covering, and the bees were just behind it.

The bees were aggressive, and I saw them chase after some children that were playing outside. I had to do something, but I didn't know what could be done. I then remembered my beekeeper friend and asked her for advice. She gave me the number for some professional bee removal specialists.

I called them, and a nice gentleman answered the phone. I was concerned that he might think asking him to remove my bees was a weird request. Instead, he was delighted that I called. I explained my situation, and he said he would come to my house to assess the situation.

An hour passed, and I heard a knock on my door. Three men clad in white beekeeping outfits stood outside my door. I came out to greet them and showed them where the bees were coming and going. They explained they would have to take the copper piece off my house to access the colony. They then told me that the service was free, but that they wanted the queen and all the honeycomb and honey. I thought that was reasonable. They then explained that I would need to have a contractor come and reseal my attic.

The men went to work, peeling off the decorative copper piece. It is an octagonal shape that wraps around the bay window. They slowly pulled it back, revealing a very old beehive shaped the same as the copper. It was fascinating. The hive had been there undetected for years. The men had numerous buckets and a vacuum cleaner that they used to gather up the bees.

They explained that they had a large bee farm and would relocate this hive there. They told me that my bees were outgrowing their current nest, so the queen was trying to move the colony. They dug and dug at the hive, extracting honey, honeycomb, and bees. They ended up taking around 80,000 bees and ten pounds of honey and honeycomb.

It was an impressive undertaking. These guys knew their stuff. They were surprised that none of the bees had gotten into my house as they had made their way into my attic. There was honey dripping down the inside of the attic walls.

Wow! What a mess. They left at the end of the day to relocate the swarm, and I was relieved they were taking the bees. I didn't want anything bad to happen to them. They are hard to come by in certain parts of my state, and I didn't want the population to suffer.

The next morning, I went outside to inspect the state of my house. The men had placed a plastic cover over the hole they created to get the bees. I had already scheduled my contractor to come and make the necessary repairs.

I walked outside on my front porch only to find a swarm of bees even larger than the original one. I was afraid and called the beekeepers again. They told me that the bees swarming on my house were worker bees that had been out gathering pollen to bring back to the nest. They said that they would be over shortly.

They pulled up to my house, donned their beekeeping suits again, and approached my house. They were prepared with their buckets and bee vacuum and went to work gathering up the bees at my front door. They then took a ladder and crawled into my attic from the hole they made the previous day.

They were surprised that there was another large swarm inside my attic that they needed to extract. They took their time, trying to vacuum up as many bees as they could.

At the end of job, some straggler bees in my attic were making their way into my house. I wasn't going to tolerate that, so they left some bee repellant in my attic that would help drive them out before my contractor could patch the hole.

It was quite the ordeal, but in the end, it was a new and interesting experience.

PICKLES

I mentioned earlier that I had a large (for a suburban backyard) vegetable garden for most of the year. It yields plenty of vegetables for Al and me, and I always have a freezer or two filled with frozen okra, green beans, etc.

I began gardening with my grandmother, Catherine, when I was a young girl. She was the sweetest person I have ever met in my life. She called me "my darling Queen Victoria" since she and my mother were from a small town in England. She had the nicest accent and gentle ways. She taught me how to prepare the soil and plant seeds and how to water the garden. We had a lot of fun together.

When I was young, we had a large patch of wild blackberries. My grandmother, mother, and sisters would grab five-gallon buckets and head off to the patch, spending hours picking blackberries and talking and laughing. Over time, as our own families grew, I brought my daughter, and my sisters brought theirs, so the tradition continued.

When we got home, we washed and sorted our berries before making cobblers, jams, and pies. It was glorious. We were all becoming quite good at preparing the sweets. Each generation taught the next how to bake.

I started planting my own vegetable garden when I was nineteen, beginning with a small patch of land in the backyard. I tried my hand at many different vegetables. Over the years I have planted cucumbers, okra, potatoes, onions, green beans, peppers, and tomatoes. I planted these in the spring, and then broccoli, cabbages, brussels sprouts, and cauliflower in the fall and winter months.

I harvest so many vegetables, especially cucumbers, that several years ago my sister Laurie taught me how to make pickles. She started me out with a simple recipe that I have perfected. I make crunchy dill and delectable bread and butter pickles along with pickled okra.

My favorite day is a Saturday in the summer when it's time to make pickles. I have read recipes as a hobby for years, so I have incorporated many new ideas into my pickle recipes.

I store the bottles in my pantry and give them away for Christmas presents or housewarming gifts, etc. People put their orders in with me far in advance so they will be guaranteed a bottle of yummy, pickled creations. I have also branched out and now make salsa and various marinara sauces. I love to cook!

Many years ago, when I was first married, I didn't know how to cook. I think I could fry an egg and make toast, but that was it. My mother gave me a copy of a popular cookbook, but as I read it, I just got confused.

I tried hard to cook dinners that were appealing, but they were burned or seasoned terribly. My husband just started taking me out to dinner instead of enduring another meal fixed by my hand. I was humiliated. His last wife was a "fabulous" cook, and my husband told me about it ad nauseam. I tried to mimic some of the recipes that he would tell me she made. They always turned out horrible.

Finally, while in line to check out at the grocery store, I noticed a beautiful cooking magazine. The front cover touted that they could teach me how to make a gourmet meal in thirty minutes. What the heck! Anything had to be better than what I had been cooking.

I purchased the magazine and took a seat on a bench in the store while I investigated this "thirty-minute gourmet dinner" recipe. To my surprise, the recipes were for a complete meal with step-by-step, easy instructions. I was excited! Maybe this was the answer to my cooking woes.

I quickly picked up the necessary ingredients and hurriedly drove home. I couldn't get in the house fast enough to begin cooking. I had about an hour before dinner would be expected to be served, or we would go out to eat again. I began assembling the different courses and started to cook.

To my surprise, the recipes worked, and the food was not only delicious, but also beautiful. Pictures were included so that I would know how to serve the yummy creations I made! Maybe I was going to be a chef after all. My mother was not a good cook, and I feared I had the same issue. Not anymore.

I went to the store the next day and bought up all the available step-by-step cooking magazines. I also employed a Creole woman to help with the housework and care for my newborn daughter. She would watch me struggle to cook dinner and finally told me to stop. She went on to show me how to make the most basic food taste delicious.

I cooked with her and learned how to put different ingredients together to alter the taste of certain dishes. I still make many of the dishes that she taught me. I make her fried chicken and her gravy and send a prayer of thanks for her. I can still hear her steady voice as she patiently taught this nineteen-year-old kid to cook!

Now I entertain quite a bit and love to turn out scrumptious meals for my family and friends. I always make more than is necessary so that I can send some home with my guests. Yes, they all get a jar of pickles too, if they want one.

FEAR

My husband and I were traveling and had a connecting flight. I was patiently waiting to board our flight when I was overcome with the most dreadful feeling of fear. I was looking at my phone to retrieve my reservations when, out of the corner of my eye, I saw pink tennis shoes almost touching my shoes. I looked up to find a beautiful girl, maybe twelve years old, standing very close to me. She was wearing neat clothes and a large backpack.

It was obvious that she was the source of the fear. I began looking around, and a large man was talking obnoxiously and loudly to the person at the ticket counter and summoning a woman to come forward with tickets. The woman was dressed in very loud colors and was wearing a strange wig that made her stand out.

I was curious and continued to watch the man flailing his arms as he talked with the agent. It was quite the spectacle.

The young woman next to me was intently watching the man too. I whispered to her and asked if that was her father. She turned to me with anger pouring from her face and whispered, "NO."

The man looked over in my direction and yelled at me to stop talking to the girl. I was unafraid.

I whispered to her again and asked if she was in trouble. She again turned toward me and whispered, "No speak English."

I continued to watch as the man and the woman ushered two young boys and the girl next to me onto the plane. I lost track of the girl. I had such a sick feeling in my gut that I couldn't keep silent. That child was in trouble.

I decided to write a text message explaining what I had seen and that I suspected that the man and the woman were involved in human trafficking. I described all the players as best I could and showed it to a flight attendant. The flight attendant buzzed around the plane and recruited the other attendants to locate the man, woman, and three children.

She came back and said they had located them and that the airline would take care of it. As she finished telling me that, I looked to my right and there was the man, two seats behind me, glaring at me.

I tried to relax on the flight, but it was impossible. I was so scared for those kids.

We landed at our destination and waited for a while to deplane. I didn't know what was taking so long, but then the flight attendant who had listened to my story called me to the front of the plane.

I quickly complied and was ushered out of the plane where there was a long line of police officers. The officer in charge asked me to tell him my story. He was very polite and reassured me they would take care of the situation. I then said that I had to go. I did not want to be around when they questioned the man. They understood, and I ran toward the taxi lane, texting my husband where I was.

I couldn't get it out of my mind, and I was worried for the children.

Finally, I couldn't stand it, and I called the airline and asked for an update. I told them what had happened, and I wanted to know if they had apprehended the man and woman and confiscated the children.

After a time on hold, a woman came to the phone and told me that they had arrested the man and woman and that the children were in protective custody while authorities located their parents.

I was so relieved and happy for the kids. If you see something, say something!

CYCLE OREGON

My husband Al and I met on Match.com in 2006. We dated a few times, and I really liked him. Then I made the mistake of asking an attorney friend if he knew Al, and he said that he did and that I shouldn't date him because he was "weird."

He was really adamant about me not seeing Al and managed to scare me, so I didn't see Al again. It then became apparent that the friend had an ulterior motive that had nothing to do with Al. He wanted to date me.

I let it go and didn't hear from Al for a year or so, and then I got a text message from an unknown number. The text read, "Victoria, would you give me another chance?" Wow! How sweet, but I didn't recognize the number.

I texted back, and Al replied. I was so happy that he texted me after I dumped him. I felt embarrassed, but I agreed to meet with him.

It happened that I had closed on a house and was moving in that night. I told Al that he was more than welcome to visit but said I would be busy. He agreed to come over to my new house.

He greeted me dressed in an impeccable Italian suit! He looked smokin' hot! He also brought me two dozen white roses, wine, and dinner from a local restaurant. He certainly had my attention.

I realized that I hadn't unpacked my wine opener or silverware yet, so Al went to the neighbor and asked to borrow the items. By the time he returned, I had found some glasses and plates.

We sat on the floor and used moving boxes as our table. I found a bucket for the flowers and centered them on the "table."

We had a great time! Since my bed wasn't set up yet, he said I could spend the night at his house. So I did! We have been together ever since.

Al had been an avid cyclist for years, and I rode occasionally. There is a lake close to my house, so we began riding around it. I was in terrible shape and was miserable at first, but then as I got stronger, I loved it!

We began riding every morning at six, six to seven days a week. I got stronger and my endurance grew. I was proud of myself and the weight loss that I was also experiencing.

Al wanted to begin riding in group rides on the weeknights and weekends. I've always had an issue with anxiety in crowds, so I was apprehensive. Al kept insisting, though, and I finally agreed to ride the hardest local ride that was available. (I didn't know that it was hard, but I sure found out.)

The course that we ride every day doesn't have many "hills" (what cyclists call actual hills, but it can also mean tall, steep mountains! I found that out the hard way too.)

The ride day arrived, and my anxiety was off the charts. I insisted that we be the last to take off so that I could avoid another cyclist.

We ride road bikes, so our shoes are clipped into the actual pedals. This gives you more power because you push down and then pull up, using your whole leg to move forward. I was new to this way of riding, so my confidence wasn't great. I feared falling while being attached to my bike.

The ride went well. The course had some steep "hills," so I had to learn how to ride them on the fly!

We finished, and I was proud of myself. Because I wanted my confidence to grow, I signed us up for many local rides so that I could gain more experience.

Al had been telling me of a ride that he had done many times called "Cycle Oregon," a seven-day ride in the Oregon hillsides. I had been to Portland many times with Al to see his mother and had fallen in love with Oregon. Al told me that you slept in tents every night after the day's ride. You would be served food in a makeshift kitchen and dining tent. It didn't sound too great to me; I like my creature comforts.

We kept riding many local rides, and Al set us up a training schedule so that we would have the strength and endurance to tackle "Cycle Oregon."

The first year we were together, Al rode "Cycle Oregon" without me. I missed the deadline to enter, so he went alone. I was miserable. Not only did I miss him, but I was also jealous that I didn't have the challenge of riding that course. I continued to train by myself and some cycling buddies that we met along the way. Al kept sending me daily reports of his experience on the ride. I kept training and promised myself that I was going to ride the course the following fall.

We rode outside as much as possible, weather permitting, and when we couldn't ride outside, we both rode our bicycles on indoor trainers. I had become so excited and motivated to ride "Cycle Oregon."

I downloaded the course and studied it carefully. One thing I noticed was that, for a fee, they would provide the tent. They would also carry your bags and tent and set them up at the next rest stop. We both opted in for that.

Another thing I noticed was that you showered in semi-trailers. This was hard to imagine, but Al reassured me that it would be fun. He also casually mentioned that they had no bathrooms, only Porta Potties to use for the whole week. I was used to that on our local courses, but for a whole week? It was dizzying to consider participating in this camping/cycling adventure.

Al had been a salesman for IBM before he became a lawyer, so the sales pitch was on. It was fun to hear all his stories of funky adventures that he had riding "Cycle Oregon."

Eventually I was hooked and decided to purchase a duffle bag and all the other items I might need for such a camping trip. We were both getting excited about the ride, and we put in many miles each month to build our mileage before the big day.

THE BIG DAY!

We shipped our bicycles to the starting point of "Cycle Oregon," so that worry was solved. We packed up all the necessary clothing, assembling each day's outfit and zipping them up in two-gallon Ziplock bags, so there was no guesswork when we pedaled out at 6 a.m. as to what we were going to wear and where it was located.

The weather was spotty, with rain showers and sleet forecasted. We had purchased rain gear to use in case of bad weather and extra layers of jerseys to combat the cold wind and sleet. I was apprehensive about the potential difficult weather conditions, but I felt we were ready.

Al packed up an inflatable mattress so we would be more comfortable in what he called "luxury camping." That would come back to haunt him.

We flew to Portland a few days before the ride so that we could visit Al's mother, and then we took a train five hours to the campground and the beginning of the ride. A few days before the ride, I started to develop a dry, hacking cough. I ignored it, focusing on the ride and the task at hand.

We arrived at the campground, which was situated in a cow pasture of tall grass and uneven terrain. The wind was biting, and dust flew everywhere. My cough began to get worse.

We strove to climb a small incline to the tent where we retrieved our entry packets containing our tickets to the meal tent, etc. We were given our tent number, and a few young men from the local football team helped us carry our duffle bags to the tent.

Walking up to the tent, I had to climb over a "cow patty" (in other words, a pile of cow poop). As I looked around the field, the wind was blowing, and there was poop everywhere. This was luxury camping? I was furious with Al. I had expected a nicer arrangement and wasn't prepared to handle this situation.

Unfortunately, I threw a fit and acted inappropriately. I had to walk off and gather myself. I felt bad. We trained hard for months, and Al was so excited that I was going to join him and ride this special ride with him. I calmed down and apologized for my behavior, then I jumped in and unpacked our duffle bags to prepare for the beginning of the ride.

It was time for dinner, so we went to a large tent where the meals of the day were offered. The food was surprisingly good, and there was plenty of it. I thought maybe this would end up being fun. The next morning came early, and the breakfast tent filled up fast.

The organizers arranged to provide us with pamphlets about each day's ride that included historical information about the town we were in and the one we would be in by the end of the day. It was charming. We ate and made our way back to the tent to get our cycling gear on. It was just over thirty degrees Fahrenheit.

Al started the ride, and I finally got the courage to go as well. Over the course of the seven days, the ride would entail 490 miles with many steep mountains to climb along the way. It was the hardest thing I have ever done in my life.

We rode the seventy to ninety miles a day, got cleaned up in the shower trucks, changed, and ended up in another tent or open area for the night's festivities. Each town on the course had arranged for events each evening—fireworks, a show put on by the local high school cheerleaders, and a Native American dance with Indian tacos to name a few. It was fun! It was so quirky, but it made the ride much more interesting.

We rode through gorgeous Oregon countryside with golden fields of wheat, or a field full of onions lying on the ground, waiting to be gathered by the local farmers. We saw various herds of cows that

I had never seen before and herds of wild stallions ran in the fields beside the road. Dust devils also spun up and down various fields.

The most majestic, beautiful experience was when we were riding into Ashland, Oregon. The tall hills were covered with thick trees, and elk jumped across the road in front of us. The sky was purple, and I thought of a phrase from "America the Beautiful": *purple mountain majesties*. I began to cry; the beauty was overwhelming.

The next morning we had to climb out of Ashland and ride fifteen miles straight up the side of the mountain. That was not fun, but we did it. At one point I was going so slow I wondered when I would just topple over the edge of the hill that was inches from my pedals. We made it up the hill, though, and on to the next town. When we came over the finish line, a big crowd handed us ice cream and a medal for finishing the course.

I cried for a while, the tears coming from a place of reverence and pride for the accomplishment, but with great gratitude as well that I'd had this experience. I will always be grateful for Al's "salesmanship" that got me to train for and participate in this great adventure. We ended up riding "Cycle Oregon" many more times and had many more magnificent experiences. Thank you, Al!

One day before riding across the Golden Gate Bridge in San Francisco, we noticed a poster for a beer commercial. It was a well-known ad, but in this one the main actor was saying, "If it requires a waiver, it's got to be fun!"

We had to sign a waiver to rent bicycles for the bridge, and then we realized that we had to sign a waiver for just about everything. So we agreed that we sure had signed a lot of waivers, and we did have fun!

I then created our "waiver book" in which I have collected copies of all the waivers we signed for various cycling events, as well as for when we went skiing, took a helicopter ride over the mountains of Maui, and rented a sailboat in Tahiti.

It's grown heavy and thick as we continue to amass reminders of all the fun we had and continue to have.

LOST!

I don't know if you have ever felt lost emotionally or spiritually. I sure have had periods where I have just felt empty and had no direction. I've always been a spiritual person, but I've had times when I've been devastated by an event, such as when I had the criminal working for me. When it was all said and done, I was spent.

My good friend Randy, whom I previously mentioned, introduced me to the teaching of David Hawkins, MD, PhD. He was a psychiatrist for fifty years but had been a spiritual teacher. I thought that I had nothing to lose, so I randomly downloaded one of his lectures. I began listening to it while riding my bicycle one morning.

The sky was yellow and orange as the sun shone through the clouds. It looked as if I were seeing heaven as I listened to Dr. Hawkins, and I was struck with an overwhelming sense of peace. I felt as if I were home as I listened to his teachings.

At one point I thought that I was so distracted by the information he was sharing that I might fall off my bicycle, so I decided to stop riding and sit in my car and listen to the rest of the lecture.

I felt like I had found the information my soul had been craving. I couldn't get enough and began listening to the monthly lectures he had given over a twelve-year period. I listened intently to each one, often many times, until the information sank in.

I was being transformed, and I felt my spirit grow. What had been an empty, hopeless person was being filled with a spiritual transformation, and joy replaced my constant anxiety. The searching and the feelings of being abandoned and lost were diminishing. I read or listened to lectures many hours a day. I couldn't get enough. I was alive again.

I began practicing his principles in my business and with my staff and patients. As I mentioned, I have been giving his very famous book *Letting Go: The Pathway of Surrender* to anyone that wanted one. Some people read it and just put it down and walked away, but many others had a transformational experience similar to mine. They were never the same.

The clinic's atmosphere began to be supercharged with positivity, and the staff seemed brighter and lighter as they performed their duties. The clinic just ran more smoothly, and the patients began commenting on how good and peaceful the clinic felt. My spirit was growing and spilling over into the clinic.

I made the decision to pray regularly in the clinic to myself and to softly play spiritual music. I wanted the clinic to be a place of peace and healing, even while a patient was receiving an aesthetic procedure.

The biggest idea that I have taken away from his teachings is "to be kind and loving towards all of life, including oneself is all that is required."

Over the years I've given away hundreds of copies of the book, and I continue to listen to and read Dr. Hawkins's messages. I am joyful. I hope that you will be curious and consider reading or listening to *Letting Go*, or any of Dr. Hawkins's other teachings.

NEW ORLEANS

My family moved to New Orleans when I was a young girl, and I consider it my hometown. Now my daughter and her family, including my five-year-old granddaughter, live there, and I visit quite regularly.

One December Al and I were in New Orleans for Christmas, and I had been looking for a house or condo there for a long time. I never found anything that was worth the money or in a good location.

My daughter had been looking with her friend, who is also a realtor. One day, I got an excited call from my daughter. She told me that she found two condominiums in the Garden District—the prettiest part of New Orleans, in my opinion. I was ecstatic. She sent me the listings and said she was on her way to look at them both. She quickly ruled one of them out but was excited about the other one.

The condo, built in 1960, is around 800 square feet with one bath, a main living area, a full kitchen, a breakfast nook, and a small balcony with an enclosed sitting area, along with a nice-size bedroom and closets. The balcony area has a sliding glass door that opens onto it and is surrounded with a great wrought-iron railing. The balcony and windows overlook the city of New Orleans.

My unit is on the seventh floor on St. Charles Avenue. You can walk out the front door and catch the streetcar. New Orleans has a great public transportation system. Having grown up there, I learned to take the streetcar and buses all over the city. I felt good that we could get ourselves around without much of a problem. The price of the unit was acceptable, but it would need to be remodeled.

I purchased the condo, and my daughter arranged for contractors to begin the remodel. I also brought my interior designer from Oklahoma City to New Orleans to decorate. I like the French flare that Barbara adds to the spaces that she designs for me, including my office and home. She was up to the task and moved through the process of picking fabrics, paint colors, etc. She assembled everything in Oklahoma City and had it shipped and installed in New Orleans. The furniture and everything were over the top. I was so happy with the design, and I feel very comfortable and safe there.

The condo is also two blocks from where Evelyn, my granddaughter, goes to school. It's very convenient for me to walk over and pick her up or drop her off at school. She loves to come to the condo and play with Gramma and Grandpa "Owl," as she calls him. We take her on the streetcar to the zoo or the aquarium or out for lunch. We have so much fun with her. She gives me so much joy!

St. Charles Avenue is the main street in the Garden District, and it's where the largest and oldest Mardi Gras parades pass by. The condominium building has a large ballroom with a nice yard in front of it surrounded by a decorative wrought-iron gate and fence protecting it from the street traffic. We take our chairs outside and can either be on the streets, begging for beads from the passing parades, or be protected by the fence in the yard.

It's a great setup! We have our own large table in the ballroom, along with other residents. Most people decorate their tables and make Creole or Cajun meals to share with everyone. I make traditional seafood gumbo and red beans and rice, to name a few.

If you get tired of the parades, you can return to the condo and take a break. The parades begin early in the morning and roll all day and into the late evening hours. We usually run into celebrity chefs that also live in the area, along with recording artists and actors. It is a fun atmosphere and a local experience rather than a touristy one.

Families buy long ladders, decorate them in Mardi Gras colors, and build a seating area for the kids on the top of them. There are thousands and thousands of these ladders all over the city. The city allows people to keep their ladders on the street for the last week of Mardi Gras, so it makes it easier for families trying to have a good time.

This part of New Orleans has a lot of huge crows. I decided to set up a feeder on my balcony so that I could feed them peanuts and grains. It did not take long before they found them. They sit on the railing and scream into the condo for me to get them some more. Evelyn thinks it's so much fun, and so do I. They tolerate our presence well, and we sit just inside the balcony and watch them.

One of my friends told me that when his daughter was young, they fed the crows as well. He told me to start asking them to bring us presents in exchange for the food. I thought that was odd, so I decided not to tell Evelyn yet. I wanted to test it and see if they would indeed bring us presents.

One of the crows was close to me, and I told him to take a peanut but that I wanted a present in exchange. I thought, *Well, no one heard me, so I'm safe from ridicule for the moment*, just in case it didn't work.

I forgot about the crows for a while, and when I returned to fill their feeder again, I noticed a six-inch piece of aluminum foil on the balcony edge. We are a long way from the street, and there was no way the wind had blown this foil up to the seventh floor. *Hmm*, I thought, *I need to test this out again*. When the crows came back, I again asked them to bring me a present.

A little while later, I went back to check on the peanut situation and see if I got another present. I opened the sliding door, and right in front of it was a beautiful leaf that was placed where a peanut had been.

I decided to tell Evelyn and see what happened. She was thrilled and had no trouble asking the crows for a present.

We patiently waited for the crows to return and see what, if anything, they would bring us. We got distracted, and when we came back to look for the crows, one of them was placing another beautiful green leaf on the railing where Evelyn had left a peanut an hour before.

How fun! So we kept feeding them and waiting for the next present. They brought us a pull tab, more leaves, and flowers. Wow! Such great memories for Evelyn and me. I can't wait to go back and see what they will leave us next time.

THANK YOU!

Thank you for hanging in there. I hope that you found my book amusing and raw!

As my patients and friends shared with me intimate situations they have encountered, I realized that I had experienced a few things that shaped me into the person I have become.

I continue to study and practice Dr. Hawkins's teachings and share the information with whomever wants it.

I will get you up to speed on where I am and what's been happening in my next book.

ABOUT THE AUTHOR

Victoria Johnson, MD, is a well-known physician in the practice of aesthetic medicine. She has pioneered many state-of-the-art laser procedures and surgeries and has helped guide the field for more than twenty years.

Dr. Johnson is a published author and has served on many medical boards and committees. She continues to teach other physicians the art of aesthetic medical practice and various medical techniques.

Dr. Johnson has won many distinguished awards, but her favorite things in life are her husband and family.